THE
MISSIONARY
KID...
TALKS

TED GARRISON

THE
MISSIONARY
KID...
TALKS

atmosphere press

To my people:
White Anglo Saxon Protestant American Zionists.
We are The Prodigal Son, and we've finally made it to
The Pig Sty. It's high time we Go Home!

Contents

Conception: A Story

I grew up in India where my parents were missionaries. In the year before I was born, my Dad was having an affair and had to get rid of Mom. My life is haunted by "sin," "adultery," "attempted murder"—being "left for dead.

My birth certificate is a letter, written by the doctor who delivered me. He used an instrument to pull me out by the head, claiming my long toes were gripping my mother's ribs. The pressure on my skull squeezed the two sides together, forming a subtle mountain range on my skull.

"To whom it may concern,

Theodore Leavitt Garrison, male, was born in the Methodist Hospital, Nadiad, on September 2, 1954, the son of American missionaries. Reverend and Mrs. John Garrison were residing at the time at Mission House, Viramgam, Gujarat."

My mother's real name was Leona Ruth Beirnes. Her parents were also missionaries, but I don't know her side of the story. My Dad's story still seems to dominate, and threaten, my outer world. Mom's story remains to be told.

When I get curious about people's religious ancestry, most American kids will claim (until interrogated), "No idea." As though they've popped into the world from nowhere, and arrived without a story or a reason. Maybe they're ashamed of something. Maybe they are the product of the secular conscience. Well then, if they happen to be White Anglo Saxon

Protestant—American Zionists, and bored to death with the current version of *that* story, read on!

Dad was having an affair with a young-single-lonely-missionary woman who lived about a hundred kilometers from Nadiad. My brother was five years older than me, and my two younger sisters were not yet born. I've tried to calculate when the attempted murder must have taken place: July or August in the year before I was born?

A determined silence pervades the whole event. As a kid I knew nothing of it except that Mom had slipped—somewhere, somehow—and had fallen down a cliff, resulting in a broken neck and a good-sized indentation in the very crown of her skull.

As new missionaries, my wife and I were on our way to Pakistan. My parents were staying, at the time, at a mission compound in Mussoorie. I had waited seven years for a convenient time to have our first conversation about "the accident."

Seven years earlier, I was in my first year of Bible College. My brother, in his post-Vietnam wandering years, visited me in my dorm room. He told me how he always "walked point" into the jungles, and went on a lot of "recognizance missions." Picking up dead American soldiers was probably the most dangerous assignment. But what he really wanted to tell me was the truth about Mom's accident. "Mom did not fall off a cliff—Dad pushed her over," he said. "It happened above Woodstock School, at the top of the hill along the 'chakr' somewhere." I would attend Woodstock School from grades seven through twelve.

So I was able to finally ask my Mom, "What really happened?" She shared as much detail as she could, and then—like one of those events, "Where were you... for Kennedy... The Twin Towers," —with the hint of a grin, she turned to me, the heavy glow of an orange sunset on her face, and said: "When the body-cast came off, you were conceived in a fit of reconciliation!" The words were so well chosen, and I imagined she must have rehearsed them. "What will I tell Ted, when we finally have to talk? You're 'a fit of reconciliation.' And the shock of… 'when the body caste came off.' I was mystified. It felt tangible, as though I had just been handed the theme of my movie.

****

Not three months after this conversation with my Mom, I fled in failure from the mission field in Pakistan. And did it in a Biblical fashion. I had left for the "Mission Field," leaving Canada for Pakistan, addicted to pornography; and pornography was not available (to me) in Pakistan. I was panicking and pushing boundaries. I just had to run—whatever. I fled from Jesus. Fled my missionary ancestry, fled my new bride, fled India and Pakistan, and headed straight for the porn shops on 42nd Street in New York. I was carrying a ton of repressed sexual/lust energy. I've had to learn how to live a secret life, more than once, in different ways. Were you ever addicted to bursting out on the street? As I was?

I think I made a thousand anonymous phone calls before caller ID was invented (the single fastest cure for any addiction). Anonymity is essential in the disease of a sex addict, and intermittent reinforcement is the most powerful form of conditioning, as I would learn when I studied psychology—really searching for understanding. Though I was a sex addict, I didn't call it that at the time. I was the sinner Dad said I would become. It all started when I knew: I can't stop "Jonny." Asking Jesus for help seemed to make my suffering worse.

Over the years, struggling to understand the energy of lust, my interest was led to psychology and psychotherapy. But this meant, deliberately for me, putting Jesus and The Bible out of focus. Don't think that's an easy transition, given the kind of missionaries we were. After many forms of education, accounted here, I've come to the conclusion that I have a nature that's right for me. Religious principles have yet to guarantee the rights of *individual integrity—or what that means.* As a child, I was told my erection was the proof of sin; so (of course) I went on to live a life of sin. An encounter with The Human Design System revealed my nature (in this world). I can say I have a nature, and it's not sinful—though full of "Detriments!" In fact, I was born in a state of "Detriment!" But that's not bad, or sinful!—it's correct for me! Wrestling with the concept of sin has never diminished in my interest.

I became fascinated by human hell realms, in the experiences of the people I met in therapy. Somehow it always felt natural to be OK with whatever people brought, and bring them to the body. Today I accept myself as I am, and, miraculously, love what it is to be me. I have a formula now that helps me better understand my feelings, and a way to make amends for my errors.

Though I'm not a story teller, this is my attempt. Stories are for us all; they are meant to be shared! And they will mean to kill us when we keep them in secret! Finally, I love the fact that we humans are vulnerable to reason, logical patterns that can be experimented with, and improved. There's a linguistic formula in here that, I think, will blow your mind.

2

The Slaughter House

Dad had found an old stone-built shack on the outskirts of Nadiad. The Muslims in the area had used it as a "slaughter house." Perhaps no one in the area would have lived in a slaughter house, but Dad was not afraid of such things. He was more eager to warn them of eternal torment, and so, of turning attention to Jesus.

There is a dark, nightmarish quality from my first three years. I can see a grey dimness within the house, the bars of a crib, or of windows, a sense of dread. As a boy I have awful memories of watching cattle, marked with red paint—destined for slaughter and beaten mercilessly as they stumbled toward death.

My parents kept the secret—the attempted murder—to themselves. When they discovered that they had conceived a child, I became for them a sign of forgiveness and love. I still wonder: What is a child conceived in a terrible secret? A child of shame? A child of love? Who am I?

Dad could be away for days, preaching from village to village, leaving Mom alone with us two boys. We were on the edge of a deep jungle, and wild cats came into the house. An enormous black dog we had would kill them—so I heard. He'd corner them, and then sit there, frozen; when they'd relax, he'd grab them by the neck and shake them to death. Perhaps the first distinct image, in my life, is that of a dog flying through the air (after a chapati).

Dad was tormented by guilt, and he could only endure it for three years. The Scriptures tell us, "Confess your sins to one another, that you may be healed." But when Dad finally did confess to the head of the mission, there would be no conversation, no talk of forgiveness. He was ordered to "Leave India, with your family—and never come back." I was three years old, going on four.

Here begins my first sense of a conscious progression of memories. Perhaps we need to be thinking before we can have access to memory. Perhaps children under four do not think. Anyway, we boarded a cargo ship in Bombay and sailed for New York City. The following is a fable told me about the journey we made as the only passengers on a cargo ship. My sister Margi got sick, and I suddenly worried that she might die. Apparently, I asked Mom, "What'll happen to Margi if she dies?"

Mom said something to the effect, "Margi's too young; God wouldn't punish a child so young—and send them to hell."

Teddy, you must have been thinking then because you asked, "Well then, what if I died?" After all, I was a year and a half older than my sister.

"Well, Teddy, we can make sure, right here and now, that you'll be with Jesus if you die. Would you like to ask Jesus into your heart?" I did. It's always good to feel safe.

When the ship docked in New York, sometime late at night—and we disembarked—I remember a kind of nausea crept over me as we traveled in a taxi through downtown New York City. In the orange night light of the inner city, I caught a glimpse of a body lying on a sidewalk. Dead people on the streets of America?! Apparently, he was "just a drunk," someone "passed out." Bombay had felt, briefly, wonderful to me, natural; but New York felt like a real nightmare. Perhaps I'd created a contrast—in my mind—with the expectation that we'd be "returning" to the land where Jesus came from. Mom reminded me, years later, how I started demanding that we "turn around and go back to India!"

****

We lived somewhere in Massachusetts, and Dad took us to see the Mayflower. I have a sense of being in his arms as he pointed to the ship, telling me about my ancient grandparents, "The famous Austins, our ancestors, came to America on that ship." He would tell us about how a later generation would walk to Missouri as missionaries to the Osage people. Along the way, one of the wagons fell through river ice. I think someone drowned and they lost a lot of stuff. My father had inherited writings and old newspaper clippings referencing this period. I read that the young Osage were "tall and naked and dirty," and how they were bathed and dressed properly, and taught how to read the Bible in English at the residential school where my ancestors served as missionaries.

I don't remember anything else about that year in Massachusetts. I think I can see jumping on a spring mattress at a dump near our house. And there's a hint of adventure, seeking treasures, like Indian dung beetles, in the dump. Maybe there was a fire in the basement and Dad put it out. But Dad couldn't stand living away from India. And the burden of the call of God on his life: "Proclaim the Gospel of Jesus to India," would not go away. "India, O India," I often heard him say. He became convinced in his spirit that, with or without support, he must return to India. While realizing they knew of the adultery and attempted murder, he informed our supporters of his intentions. We did find a little Christian And Missionary Alliance church in Owen Sound, Ontario, Canada, willing to continue supporting us. In faith we headed back to India. Bombay. Now Mumbai.

We had only money enough to live in an apartment overlooking the slums. It was noisy; the cinema music was unquenchable; I heard screaming, sometimes extended and horrifying.

I heard the screams of women who (I was told) would douse themselves in kerosene and burn themselves to death, screaming for the world to hear. The relentless pounding of "masala" from overhead and below. It came from everywhere. Fantastic shows could happen in the open area that centered the apartment buildings. A man rode a bicycle around, day and night, for at least a week, trying to break the world record. He ate and pooped and peed on his bike. I remember how he wobbled at the end, but I didn't see him finally fall. And then the miracle at 4:30 AM, when I'd get up to pee. Returning to bed, I'd look out an open window and see the few dim orange lights— the quiet stillness was unbelievable, mysterious, a miracle destined for a shattering.

****

Dad met a Sikh named Bhakta Singh Chabra, who had a conversion experience to tell as great as St. Augustane. He came upon a Punjabi language New Testament—thrown, apparently, from the sky to the sidewalk in front of him. He glanced at it, and counted it a miracle. This was a book with a personal message he had not imagined! He read it through feverishly— and determined that he'd been called, like St. Paul himself, to establish Christian "Assemblies."

As Bhakta Singh continued to read the Panjabi New Testament, he too was called "by The Lord" to follow the New Testament instructions for establishing Churches. The instructions were abundantly clear in the writings of St. Paul!

Based solely on the authority of his having found a New Testament on a sidewalk, he cut off his uncut hair, and began converting people to Jesus, and by the hundreds. He did this without any help from foreign missionaries! In fact, he had already started about a hundred (so I heard) "Assemblies" before he met Dad. Now Dad was a man steeped in the New Testament, and passionate to share in its interpretation. Dad was soon preaching publicly with Bhakta Singh. The Bhakta Singh Assembly was my first remembered experience of Church.

Bhakta Singh and his "saints" met on Sundays in available Public School buildings. There were three consecutive services, every Sunday. The men sat on one side, women on the other. First we sang for a full hour. Then two or three elders would preach for an hour or more, depending on how the spirit moved them. The preaching was followed by another hour of communion. And finally, we had a huge feast, sitting on the floor and eating off the huge leaves from the "peepul" trees. Chairs were nonexistent. The thin straw mats dug into the skins of my ankles. The singing went on and on. I can still hear "O O ka ka ra." Bhakta Singh used popular cinema tunes, the ones we heard from megaphones that hung from telephone poles. The ubiquitous cinema music! He put those popular tunes to Bible verses. I can still see the blood vessels in Dad's neck, bursting with song, the tears streaming down his face. He cried freely (which embarrassed me) whenever he talked about forgiveness and the love of Jesus. When we toured, while on furlough, we inspired our supporters with our hymn singing. Dad also played the saw. He played it so beautifully! I have often wondered why we don't hear more musical saws! It's a great instrument!

We were experiencing India in a way that few missionaries had, with their bungalows, gardens, and servants. We didn't see other white people, and soon we would attend the huge Bombay Public School, and problems for my brother, and a new problem for my parents.

Missionary Business

They said it as a joke, but it's true: I failed kindergarten. And I think I know why. We had moved again to a part of Mumbai called Juhu Beach. In distress the teachers would call my parents to tell them how I refused to come into the classroom, running away from them on the playground. I don't remember running away, but I do remember coming into the building at nap times. I think I came in for the teacher who patrolled the area. I always picked my lying down spot deliberately, at the border of the other napping children. Every time she walked by, I hoped to catch a clearer glimpse of her legs from under her dress. What was there, in that darkening area? I don't remember seeing underwear, but it felt as though we had a relationship. Perhaps she knew what I was up to, walked even closer to me, and perhaps lingered. I could run away from that teacher, but I could not avoid a bottomless curiosity for looking up her dress. I have a series of scene suggestions for Norman Rockwell. This is one of the earliest.

****

Human beings are curious about differences, and pick on them. I don't remember anything bad done to me, but apparently the Indian boys had forced themselves on my brother in an effort to see what his white (circumcised) penis looked like.

My parents compromised and started looking for a school that would be safe for innocent missionary kids. They soon learned of Sunrise School, located in Nasik, one of the holiest of Hindu cities in India. About fifty evangelical missionary kids lived with their dorm parents.

Sunrise School was in a square, ten or so acres in area, hemmed in by a cactus and barbed wire fence. A large school house was just inside the front gate. On either side of the school building were sports fields, and the whole back area was used for play and sports. On the other side of the school building there were paths edged with hedges, monkey bars, a huge swing set, and more trees to climb. Two dorm buildings, boys on one side and girls on the other, were separated by a dining hall, the real center of the school. To one side was a large maintenance shed, which we used as a base for flashlight beacon and kick-the-can. Two or three other small buildings were available for music classes and other class activities. Low hedges ran everywhere around the drive and walkways. A massive banyan tree grew next to the front gate. Its lower branches ran parallel to the ground, and we ran along them in games of "tree tag." In front of the boys' dorm was another large tree with a tree fort and a rope swing. It's amazing to me that tree climbing wasn't banned. Two or three kids a year fell out of trees, breaking arms and legs. Perhaps because we were in India, where fate—not law—predominates. In the back field, we boys built a shack out of sticks. I remember a sense of magic, the protective feeling of being inside something that you helped to build. I loved the sense of secrecy our little hut provided. We are in here, and they are out there.

****

My parents took turns dropping me off at Sunrise. It was Mom who took me the first time. Maybe this was my first conscious "primal scream" event. We arrived at the school in the afternoon, but it was not until evening when she left. I was lying on a single jut rope bed, lined up next to the opening to the bathroom. Mom and my sister (still a preschooler) were getting ready to leave. The lights were out:

My sister Margi is standing by my bed. I can see Mom standing in front of a dresser and combing her hair, her dark image framed by the door to the screened-in veranda. I send Margi as my messenger—"tell Mom not to go." Margi comes back saying, they "have to go." I ask her again, pleading, and she walks over to Mom with the message.

Mom never did come over to say goodnight. She told me, years later, that she "just couldn't"; her sadness and her tears would have burst over me. What would it have been like to have held my weeping mother? Maybe that would have been really terrible.

When they did walk away into the night, I gathered up my blankets and snuck up the hall to my brother's room, where I slept on the cement floor beneath his bunk bed. I heard the wailing cinema music and wondered what the new feelings were. When I hear Indian music today, I still feel melancholy. In the morning, a miracle happened. My loneliness evaporated when I discovered happy connections with other white boys just like me.

The next year at Sunrise, it was Dad's turn to drop me off. We must have already said goodbye, as I was in bed, where the memory begins. I must have thought he'd already gone, that I wouldn't see him again for months. But then I heard the sound of his voice as he walked down the path in front of the dorm. He was chatting happily with another adult (the woman he would marry after Mom died). I remember that he was laughing. I leapt from my bed and crossed the hallway to the screen door. Next to the screen was a clay murdka (large water container), and across from the murdka, on the wall behind, hung our tin cups, each cup with a name painted in red. I stood there, surprised consciously by my helplessness—

right at my deepest need. I couldn't cry out; though he was so close, I could have crashed through the screen and into his arms. But I stood there, absorbed in a sadness I had not imagined. I remember the effort I had to make to stand there in utter silence, holding down the sounds of my wracking sobs.

****

Missionary kids are required to learn the importance of what their parents are doing. Missionaries are called by God to the borders of hell. There they warn the heathen-lost of imminent danger. Only God can call someone to The Mission Field. A missionary is one who, with the zeal of a terrorist, gives his life for what he believes. There are no Christians like missionary Christians. It is the missionary who challenges the faithful, back home, regarding the cost of discipleship, and what it means to "take up the cross of Christ": daily devotions, memorize the Scriptures, put Jesus first in all things, confess your sins, attend all Church activities, evangelize the unsaved in your own neighborhoods, etc. Pray without ceasing.

Our teachers at Sunrise always reminded us that our parents were "doing God's work," which demanded all of their time. There's no place for children on the front lines of battle. Make no mistake, there is a battle, and it's real. And we were exposed to the evidence of spiritual darkness all around us. We were surrounded, but Jesus was with us.

To prove the reality of the spiritual darkness surrounding us, our teachers exposed us to the shocking, and evil, core of Hinduism: Flashy posters of Kali, covered in gore, her tongue sticking out, dripping with blood. I felt impressionable and wanted to understand why the pictures made me feel sickly fascinated. I gazed at those flashy-fleshy posters, the reflecting reds and blacks and blues and greens, depicting Hindu gods in violent acts, the mangled bodies of their victims dropped and dripping from teeth and hands, and crushed under foot.

We were not provided an explanation or commentary on the pictures. But we were shown the obvious horror and gore. (I learned, years later, that the image of Kali, with her tongue sticking out, depicts her at the very moment when She's suddenly made aware, in the momentum of her rampage, of having just gone too far: in slicing off Shiva's head! Shiva was saved—since he can't really be killed—by the head of an Elephant, and became Ganesha. The bloody tongue is the sign of Kali's self awareness. She can go too far! Remember that, man. If you own a Kali without the tongue sticking out, beware, she's still on a rampage, and you could be next!)

It was, therefore, impressed on us that people who worshipped such images must be lost ,and living in sin and darkness. Here was the very reason why Jesus died on the cross. So, after viewing the terrifying Hindu gods, we were directed to shift our gaze to the sufferings of Jesus on the cross. This was the only image that could save us from a sinful world. We were to see how He suffered such violence in order to save us. Jesus—beautiful savior! See the blood flowing from His side. Feel the depth of His love for us, boys and girls; and also for the heathen—the lost—"the unsaved are all around us." I heard the haunting music from down-town Nasik, and imagined people in dark temples, worshipping the gory images. Lying on my cot every night, I felt enveloped in an incomprehensible spiritual battle. The Bollywood sound track only deepened my trance.

****

I remember the dorm room the night I came down with diphtheria. I didn't know I was sick, but awoke to the roar of battle, thunderous and close and loud. Opening my eyes, I saw—clearly—hairy, monkey-like demons flying through the air, high in the rafters. Now and then, one of them swooped down at me with a grimace, pitchfork in hand. They flew so directly at me, I instinctively ducked under my covers to avoid them. It occurred to me that the horde of demons were all in flight, driven through the dark space above me.

Far off, to the left and beyond the walls, I could see, or clearly sense, the presence of Jesus on a translucent white horse—charging through the air with its thundering hoofs. The horse seemed to have wings. Though I could make out the horse and its thunderous charge, I couldn't see Jesus. The horse kept coming, but where was Jesus? In alarm, I woke up my roommates and declared, "Armageddon has begun! Wake up!" They lifted their sleepy heads and looked at me—dully—and went back to sleep. But when the roar of battle persisted, I yelled at them. "Listen! The battle of Armageddon—can't you hear it!" The other kids grew worried and ran to get the dorm parents. I couldn't settle down! Wasn't it obvious—why didn't they hear and see what was going on?

The next thing I remember was lying in the back of a jeep. Someone was driving me through the night to a mission hospital in another town many miles away. I was kept isolated for a month in a little shack behind the hospital. I had daily—it must have been painful, because I remember injections in my bottom. There were quite a few books on a book shelf, and my first sense of intrigue for the materiality of "a book," the mysterious heft of the thing... that they each carried a mystery that I might one day discover. I felt lonely in a way that never went away.

****

The classroom at Sunrise School provided my first practical lessons in fear management. Every single class, from grade one to grade twelve, was, for me, a practice in fear management. Any classroom is a threatening place for me, even still. The first time I saw a Charlie Brown cartoon, I laughed so hard when I heard the sounds the teachers made in Charlie Brown's head: Mra, mbra mra mra mra mbra—that was it! I heard every question like that. Mrra mumum mrrarra? I could easily recognize the individual words, but the question itself would turn into thickets in my head. On top of feeling strangely deaf, I learned of the consequences for bad answers. The pressure felt enormous, and inexplicable. Why?

During one of my first days in the classroom at Sunrise, I began to interrogate myself. It was a problem I couldn't tell anyone about, and I had to figure it out on my own. I really thought: for someone to feel this scared it must be the fear of death itself.

I can tell you now, that before the trip to Sunrise School, Dad had an initiation experience for me. He took me into the slaughter house, where I could witness—he had arranged it—the up-close slaughtering of a cow. Some men, as fast as they could, roped the cow's legs and shoved it over. Right away, a man with a big sword slashed straight down at the neck. I saw the gash, which only cut to the spine. And before I could see more, I turned and sprinted, vomiting, toward the door. The classroom setting brought back that similar, nauseating sensation, like something terrible was happening.

So I wanted to know if the teachers were going to kill anyone, or me, for doing something bad. To find out, I'd have to hide somewhere in the classroom, where I'd be overlooked. Near to the back but not all the way back, slightly off to the right side of the classroom, but not all the way over, and always behind someone. I kept that position through twelve years of school, on the left or right side... and never once raised my hand to answer a question! I trained every single teacher on how futile it was to ask me a question. I could never have the right answer, and I refused to guess and be wrong.

I learned that rulers were used for spanking, and that sometimes kids were made to stand in the corner—as happened to my sister when she failed to memorize a Bible verse. She just stood in the corner, wailing loudly, on and on, and

I felt terrible for her, but they didn't kill her. That was all I really wanted to know for sure. As long as I knew they wouldn't kill me, the fear was manageable. So what if I don't have any answers!

Even so, what really accentuated my fear was having to go to the chalk board. Hell might be fire and brimstone, but standing, frozen at a chalkboard, might be worse. I must have cheated every time, widening and straining my eyes without moving my head. I could hide behind others in class, but going to the board was torture. I didn't know the answer to anything, and imagining an answer felt insane—yet the only way forward. Thank God for ball-park answers. Or I would strain my eyes without moving my head, looking to the left or right, hoping to catch the glimpse of an answer. In fact, if I did see what looked like the answer, "5," for example, I would write "6." I didn't care about having the right answer, just the resemblance of one. Maybe cheaters are, first of all, ashamed of limitations. Maybe I'm math and grammar dyslexic. Anyway, I came to the realization, that while I might be punished for not knowing, or for misbehaving, at least they wouldn't kill me. What a relief! Like a scientific experiment: I had proved to myself that my fear—in the moment—was unfounded. Is there a monster around? Then look under the bed! Today, when I feel anxiety, or nervousness, I ask myself: Is there a chance I could die, and if there doesn't seem to be, then I know I'm not afraid, but suffering from useless mental anxiety, or I'm nervous about a relationship conflict. And if I am threatened with the fear of death—run! Punch! I've done that too, I'll tell you.

****

Sin followed my brother and me to Sunrise School: Sex play. Sex play at Sunrise School consisted of a quick giggle or tug of another boy's penis, or taking a peek, with the girls, at our— very different—private parts. In the dorm, after lights out, we boys played "milking the cow." We took turns being "the farmer" while the rest of us got down on our hands and knees, and lined up to be "milked." We'd laugh and run back to bed. I don't think we knew what an orgasm was. Most of us quit this activity by grade three, but there were rumors that a couple of the boys kept doing it. I guess that's about the right ratio. I just wanted to wrestle with the boys; but there was something fascinating about the girls. I would sit in class behind a girl and marvel at how some girls' hair-cuts, from the back, appeared to me in the shape of my erect penis, only very large. I stared at the crease and the curl, so well placed around the neck—the girls all had the same haircut! This was exciting and troubling for me—how vivid an image: the head of my penis, only huge, and each head a little different.

What I really wanted to see was a girl's private parts, what it looked like. This was an interest shared by a few other boys. One day, it must have been a Saturday, I helped organize a "peek show" with an equal number of boys and girls. We made a "no touching" rule. About eight of us agreed to play. We met behind a shack in the back field. My memory of this is like one of those "where were you when..." memories. I can see myself, bending awkwardly down, and sideways, then the glimpse of a shiny little rosy bud emerging suddenly through her puffy folds. I had a very weird feeling, as though I felt more scared than excited about what I'd seen.

Someone told on us. The only consequence was a brief scolding. I was relieved, and actually surprised that they didn't spank us, or worse. But can't you see another Norman Rockwell for this scene? It would have been his most famous. The boy at the front of the line, leaning sideways, awkwardly, straining to get a glimpse of a girl's clitoris while she raises her own dress and pulls down her underwear, nudging her clitoris out into the open. I can imagine the line of boys facing the line of girls, all straining to see what they were missing.

****

As for "what God wants me to do" ... In a moment of encroaching death, I had made an agreement with God. Asthma almost killed me—once a year. For three or four straight days and nights I would struggle for every breath. We had no medicine or access to emergency care. I'd lie on my bed, curled up in "the child pose," struggling for each breath. The last attack I had (when I was eight or nine), I started to become aware, in my struggle to breathe, that my mind was somehow involved in something like "the choice to breathe." Yes, it was as though I had a choice to breathe, or not! In a weird way, this thought, that I might choose *not* to breathe felt strangely empowering, and brought me this encounter with God. Totally worn out and exhausted, I found myself bargaining with God. "OK, I'm about to give up here, you can have me back. I can't keep working so hard for every breath! ... But now, it seems, I have a choice! I'm about to quit trying to breathe! Or you can heal me, and if you do, I'll be your preacher! But you have to heal me now, or I'll quit!" Well, no sooner had I made that deal with God, honestly, when a man, wearing shawl kameez clothes (I don't know why I remember that glimpse), walked into the house and gave me a tiny white pill.

I took the pill, and—almost instantly—went straight to heaven. Heaven was being able to breathe without a struggle. As I gazed down from our large Mumbai balcony—the noise, the shops, all the people—the world, as it is, was truly perfect, and incomprehensibly beautiful. I was OK, after all. Heaven felt tangibly real to me, in that moment. No awareness of suffering, no struggle to breathe: heaven! I still don't know who that man was or what was in the pill. There were no hallucinations, or colors, or distortions of reality, even if it was psychotropic. Anyway, I never had another asthma attack in my life. There's a man in India with a cure for childhood asthma!

19

Third Culture Personality

I take some comfort in my diagnosis: Third Culture Personality Disorder. We are basically missionary and military kids, raised in a so called "Third Culture." When you tell a child that they are not from the area around them, the child learns "I am not from here" (the first part of the problem) and, perhaps more importantly, "I am from somewhere else—and I don't know what that means, except that I am not from here." The disorder endures for life, as though one were an immigrant—who at least knows where they're from. TCPD's are handy people to have around, in any social situation. Humans can only gain from an alternative point of view. (Or do they?) Someone with TCPD knows something: the people around are all in cahoots with each other already; how they move through the space, how they look and sound—as though they were a single organism. They all know what to wear in the sun, partial cloud, misty or windy. When you don't feel part of the physical organism around you, *you* are the real alien. You're not from anywhere.

****

My tenth birthday is the only birthday I can remember. If I live to be a hundred, I'll repeat its significance. Dad had decided to call me "Peter," but when I was born, Mom had burst out, "What a Teddy!" I was too cuddly for "Peter"—the rock. I'll keep my rock hidden.

As I announced to the family at breakfast that I was to be called "Ted!" from now on, my two young sisters (by a year and a half, and four years) were awestruck at the sudden increase of my stature. Mom, however, seemed not to have noticed. Sometime later in the day, she called, "Teddy, come here!... Teddy! Come here at once!" ... "Teddy!" The delirious triumph of my silence: I didn't have to obey! Teddy was not my name! Failing to "come" when called was a serious offense, and had my announcement not been clear, I would have felt guilty. Now my silence was justified. She would really have to call me Ted.

****

My parents sent my brother off to live with relatives in America. They didn't have the funds, apparently, to pay the Woodstock School tuition for all four of us. Someone had to be sacrificed. They put him on a passenger ship. It was dusk in Mumbai as the huge vessel slowly pulled away from the harbor. Dad raised his voice, dramatically, and sang his favorite hymn, "Trust and Obey, for there's no other way to be happy in Jesus." He sang all the verses. I stood beside him, conspicuously frozen in place. Cupping his hands around his mouth, he projected his voice toward the ship as it slowly pulled away into the darkening sky. I felt embarrassed, as passengers on the ship gathered at the rails to listen, and sad to see my brother drifting away, hanging over the rails. It was as though I lost him that day. He would increasingly become "the black sheep" of the family, while I would become the hope of missionary continuity. After four generations of missionaries in India, it would fall on me to carry on the tradition. Little did they imagine.

A final memory from my Sunrise days involves walking with Dad through the village, which was all around the school. As Dad was prone to do, when sensing a potential crowd, he stopped to preach. He could make The Gospel sound like "FIRE!" So there was a crowd in no time, mostly kids. When he finished, we turned and started to walk away. The kids started throwing stones at us, and one struck me on the side of the head. It felt like a thud, deep under water, and I was surprised that it didn't hurt. But a lot of blood poured out! As we got back to the School, I was celebrated for having suffered persecution for my faith. I really did feel like a champion.

****

I've experienced some miracles in my life, but only one that actually touched me. During a summer vacation between Sunrise School and Woodstock School, a friend from the mission school and I rode our bikes from Nasik to Pune. The event happened toward the end of the second day of our journey. We'd spent the night in an obscure Catholic monastery on the edge of the village. Two white boys on bicycles was a spectacle. Coming into the village, a crowd of kids came running at us. We were exhausted and just wanted to know where we could lie down and spend the night. The kids knew right away how to help us. They rushed us—running along as we peddled slowly—to this little monastery compound. I did not know there were other kinds of missionaries. We were each led to a tiny monastic cell and promptly handed a bowl of plain black beans. I got my wish, eat something and lie down. The room had a bed and a cross on the wall. A poignant and deliberate silence terminated conversation. I must have slept soundly, but remember that I did wake up feeling remarkably refreshed. We got on our bikes and left without saying a word.

After cycling all day, we were ready to stop when suddenly The Ghats opened up and we were speeding downhill.

I was tired; and, after peddling for so long—on the flat—had forgotten the geometry pertaining to momentum and sharp corners. So, not far down the hill, rounding a corner, a bus was coming at me from the other direction, and I was forced to nudge to the right—away from the turn in the road and hurtling toward the edge of a cliff. The bike tires began to skid on the tiny rocks as I tried to adjust my trajectory. I managed a glance—to an unthinkable distance below—huge boulders and trees at the bottom. There was no way that I could change my direction. Talk about staring death in the face! But as I came to the edge—in the act of the launch—I was suddenly—firmly and deliberately—shoved by a force that set me upright and at the proper angle to the road! Something... the sensation of raw strength—with strong open palms—caught me, and also pressed me in the proper direction! I knew, without a doubt, that God had just saved my life. It was beyond belief—it happened to me! It had to be a miracle, and the proof that Jesus is real! He had physically intervened to save me from certain death. What happened didn't involve any faith or belief—it was done to me! I couldn't get over it.

So that's the story I told everyone. But... however... everyone around me was other missionary kids and their parents. How my fellow believers marveled at the intervention of God on my behalf! And I'd still be telling the same story— if only some wicked, unbelieving person had not mentioned, "Probably the wind coming up from the valley floor actually pushed you back on the road!" That was weird for me to understand. I felt a sinking sense of truth in the naturalistic explanation. For a while, when sharing this event with others, I'd inwardly veered from the notion of the wind, and returned to my Bible Story. It took me years to accept the truth; it felt like blasphemy. In the believer's story, God saved me; in a Godless world, the wind. The miracle remains.

****

23

We met up with David again on one of our furloughs. He'd been living with relatives in St. Paul. It was the era of "nuclear bomb threats" from Russia. We actually did climb under our desks. I didn't know if I should feel silly or afraid. But the chief difference between Sunrise School and St. Paul was the bullying and fighting. I can't imagine a "fight" occurring at Sunrise School. Sure, we used to wrestle; and we found other ways to compete with each other.

The kids at St. Paul liked to fight, just to fight. "Do you wanna fight?"

I wasn't even angry. "What do you mean, fight?"

So this kid, out of the blue, put me in a head lock. I was surprised at how determined I had to be to break his lock on my head. When I finally pushed him away, I was left with a splitting headache, shaken and nauseous.

Other boys wanted to fight me, but this bully in particular. He would order me to pass him the ball, even when he was on the other team. I managed to ignore him, until one day, walking home from school on the icy road, he snuck up behind me and tripped me to the ground. When I got up, I saw the air turn red, and without a thought, punched him squarely in the face. He fell down, bleeding; a bunch of kids looked on as I turned and walked away. The next day he came to school with a huge wrap around his head and nose. Maybe I broke his nose. No one said anything, but I was never bullied again. I'm not sure, now, how to think about that, though I hold the conviction that initiating violence is forbidden—"do no harm." I also acknowledge that natural bodily reactions can occur spontaneously and without mental interference. Maybe I agree with Bruce Lee, who said, that while he would never contemplate initiating violence, if someone came at him with the intention to kill, his own body would take over, and he might kill without a thought.

****

My sisters and I were sent to Woodstock School, located at seven thousand feet in the first range of the Himalayas. Woodstock today is considered one of the ten most elite schools in the world. And it was a great school for me. There were kids from (at least) thirty-five different nationalities. It was at Woodstock that I first noticed the difference between new American kids—and everybody else. Woodstock had a "Study Abroad" program, attracting kids from the United States ("America" to me). The American kids invariably stood out to me. They struck me as, simultaneously, arrogant, plus somehow able to pull it off. My impression of "The White American" would develop through high school. When I went to Canada, after Woodstock School, I would find a whole country of people who shared my basic impression of the White American Male—me. And then, when Donald Trump came along—there it was in full bloom, all I had imagined—in the flesh! Though George Bush had the best walk.

When vacation was over, all the missionary kids from Maharashtra gathered in Bombay for the three-day train ride to Dehra Dun, a beautiful city at the foot of the Himalayas. Train travel in India is a complete experience of India. I tell anyone interested in India: just get on a train and travel around. Every train station is a place for trade and cultural exchange between different language groups. The traveler can lose a sense of time, when the rush to destination falters. You sit back and listen, and see the world as it is. Let Mother India entertain you, and rock you to sleep. Trains in India don't necessarily follow the schedule [correction, today they do!]. Things start when they do, and you get there when they get there. The experience of just being in India, as a traveler, satisfies the essential requirements for a real spiritual pilgrimage. If you're suicidal and, still have money—go to India. If you survive, you won't be the same. If you get ripped off, you are just paying your dues.

Waking up at a station at night, the squeaking wheels

slowly halting, you become aware of all the snoring, mixed in with tubercular coughing. I wanted to laugh. You meet everyone on the train. I remember a roly-poly twenty- or thirty-year-old guy who was the very object of a god in the flesh. He was a living statue, which they washed down continuously and fed unsparingly. Even when he lay down to sleep, his mother, I imagined, mopped his brow and arranged his pillows. I didn't notice any disability. He was the spitting image of someone "served hand to foot." And he whined and complained about everything.

I was dumbfounded, and it felt repulsive. Somehow, it just seemed wrong, as his mother mirrored his complaining with her own abject exhaustion, but then kept mopping his face. Would one not revolt against the imposition of specialness? Would one not revolt against imposing specialness on another? But human "specialness" is wildly variegated. The "special" take their specialness for granted. I'm special just because I'm a White American Missionaries' Kid. The Evangelical world gives me the right to preach and tell everyone, especially Christian people, how to get right with Jesus. People like me have been given the spiritual authority to inform Donald Trump about what is going on in these end times. That's special.

Two friends, traveling back to school on the train, climbed up on the roof and were struck by a low bridge. One of them fell into the river and drowned, and the other died, right there, from the blow. My roommate was there. He said he heard the thud, and when the train stopped he saw a hand hanging limply, dripping blood. I have that image in my mind as though I was there. The death of those two boys was a shock for Woodstock School. When you live in a boarding school, you develop closer bonds than those at a day-to-day school. It was one of those shattering experiences, required of teenagers: my first encounter with the death of someone I knew well. It had the feeling of a force, drawing my mind toward another mystery: listen, ponder this, but don't expect an answer.

Taking A Stand
For Jesus

Though essentially a Christian school, Woodstock School was open to students of all religious backgrounds. In High School, I began to notice my judgments towards "liberal teachers," those I deemed to be too open-minded. Yet in seventh grade, I don't think I thought about such differences. We all just played together. The seventh and eighth grade dorm was called Ridgewood. The school was a mile away; a hike weaving back and forth up a pretty steep incline.

I shared a room with boys in the same grade. It was like a barracks; maybe it used to be. We went as a group, after "lights out," on viking-like-raids against sleeping kids in other dorms, sneaking in and clobbering them with our dhobi bags full of dirty clothes. Unlike Sunrise, I don't remember any punishments, though I do remember an attempt.

Unlike Sunrise, the teachers at Woodstock were not allowed to beat us. We tested the resolve of one poor English gentleman, kindly filling in for the dorm parent who was away on a brief weekend vacation. We made noise, or raided another dorm after lights out. Anyway, we'd made it back to our beds when he thundered in with the anger of British Royalty. He threw on the lights and, without interrogation, proclaimed that we would stand at the foot of our beds in silence for twenty minutes. This would never happen. If we made any noise at all we had to start again. It's hard to imagine a more entertaining evening—the humor, for us, at his expense, for the price of a few whacks from a tall umbrella. We would have stood there all night just to see what he'd do the next time someone snorted or coughed on purpose when he wasn't looking. This was not punishment for us, but a Monty Python skit—before it's time. Eventually, he shortened the time to ten minutes. Equally hopeless. He cut the time down to a minute, and I'm not sure he succeeded at that, or just walked away in despair. It was the suit-and-tie British sternness, a tone we loved to mimic already, that made the whole situation so funny for us. Aren't children everywhere this perverse? Today I would not kill a giant lizard, or shoot birds or monkeys for sport, and I should not mock and say, "dumb ass."

****

My relationship with Jesus got fired up in grade nine. I read somewhere that the Bible exudes Teen Age Mythology. It has all the seriousness of a passion for reality. The battle against the sins of the flesh (masturbation) inspired my Bible reading and prayer. My Dad's words had won the battle, the struggle was too real. Some of the missionary kids had lost any semblance of religion—and became hippies, grew their hair long, smoked weed, and hung out at the "chai ducan" down Teri Road. I was the champion for "The Bible Club Kids."

When I look back on this time, I'm impressed by the fact that, as a rule, I remained totally committed to being an example for Jesus. It was that simple for me. It was all about Jesus, not even God or The Father or The Holy Spirit. Dad's mantra was, "Let me see Jesus." I did not smoke weed. I did not stay out late. And I did not dance. This is all astounding to me now. No dancing... I can't imagine that! And I even rolled up marijuana leaves from the plants growing all over the hillside, but was never tempted to smoke it. Really?

The school allowed dancing on Friday nights, and it happened in the common space at the Hostel. I went to my dorm room, transfixed by the thumping that I could hear and feel. But I wrestled against it like some desert father quoting the Bible against an attack of demons.

Bonnie was my first serious girlfriend; all we did was kiss. I felt that God would let me off the hook for masturbating for now, which became a necessity, given the fruitless hours spent kissing. Our first kiss was classically bad; one of those picture-perfect Norman Rockwells. I had walked her to the girls' dorm, and we were standing under an umbrella in the rain. It seemed the right thing to do, to kiss her, so I bent toward her and kissed her quickly on the lips, smearing our lips to the side and clattering our teeth together—it was really bad. I rushed away, embarrassed, but like I'd won a medal.

****

One day on a summer vacation, probably in grade nine, I somehow came upon a magazine written for teenage Mennonite kids. It was called *WITH*. Why I remember that detail may correspond to the significance of what I announced to the family, my two sisters and Mom and Dad, that evening at supper. "I read an article in '*With*' that said masturbation isn't sin, and that the sin of Onan wasn't masturbation."

Reading that point of view was truly happy news to me, and I was not going to let it pass: that I had been tormented all my life by Dad's oppressive attitude about it: that masturbation was a sin and would lead to more sin down the road. If all this was nonsense, then I was scot free to masturbate whenever I felt like it. What a liberation! I addressed my Dad, and said, there are two things that I experience, together: I masturbate, and I feel ashamed of it—and I think, now, that feeling ashamed of myself is worse for me than the fact that I masturbated! So I'm just going to masturbate freely, and not feel ashamed! And I stuck to my guns as we argued, with Dad rifling through the Bible, finding verses that he could read with conviction. When supper ended, we continued the argument into the bedroom, where we knelt around their bed and talked. Everything St Paul had to say about lust and the flesh and the devil, and the sin of Onan again.... Finally, my Mom, her head in her hands, looking down at the bed, said softly, "O John..." That was all, just, "O John..." And it was over. I had prevailed and went straight to my room and had the first guilt-free jerk off in my life.

****

I was halfway through grade ten when my brother returned from Vietnam. But instead of reporting to where he should have been, he "went AWOL." He was not about to forego the requirement for coming back alive: "Party!" Then he just disappeared, and no one knew where he was. Mom and Dad felt they had a duty to look for him, and rescue him. The army told us that if and when he returned, he'd have to spend a month in the "Stockade" at a base in Arizona. Fortunately, Dad had a sister living in the Arizona desert north of the Chiricahua hills.

I didn't fit in at the Sun Valley High School, and I didn't try to fit in. I felt invisible, and people left me alone. I played the flute in the band. It was a long ride on the bus to School, but I didn't mind it. I was proud to get a driver's license for a motorcycle and a car. My driving test consisted of pulling out to the road, driving a block, making a U-Turn, and driving back. He should have failed me—I failed to use my blinker while pulling out on the road.

For the whole six months in Arizona, I was in a trance of getting back to India. David finally showed up with a 410 shotgun, and very bad language. He listened non-stop to Neil

Young, Janis Joplin, and Led Zeppelin. His music, late into the night as I tried to sleep, got into my bones... "I went into town to see you yesterday, but you were not at home, so I wandered off... aloooone."

We went to the closest Evangelical Church. It was there I had my first personal lesson in "race relations." I had a black friend, somehow, and went over to his house once. I invited them to Church with me, but they laughed. I was flummoxed, and questioned them. I could tell that they didn't know how to tell me something: they would not be allowed in. This I could not believe, and I argued with them. I said that's ridiculous, and that they should come with me anyway. They kept laughing at me. They convinced me that what I was asking them to do was impossible for them to do. I did not (want to) understand. Well, the first chance I had, that Sunday, I cornered the Pastor and drilled him as to why my Black neighbors wouldn't be welcomed at Church. He was apologetic; but I wished I could rebuke him, "In the name of Jesus, you have an un-Biblical attitude! Missionaries seek converts; they don't turn people away!" I was so naive: I couldn't believe that Christian people could be racist. Little did I understand... what I was. We went back to India and left David to his years of endless hitchhiking. David is the end of my American Dream—he's my American hero today with his Mexican wife.

****

A group of us missionary kids, living in Maharashtra, thought we'd take a bus down to Goa for a couple of weeks. I was still in a kissing relationship with Bonnie. Ruth, one of the rebellious girls, came with us. Meanwhile, I was eager to see naked hippies. They stayed in an old monastery on one of the many beaches. It was a renowned highlight on the global "hippy trail." My first glimpse of naked hippies was unspectacular, and I felt slightly amazed by my lack of arousal. Then, one afternoon, looking through a small clump of white hippy women, I glimpsed a skimpy blue bikini. And a body that was "sexy." As she nimbled through the naked bodies, I was captivated. Now, the empty bodies left no pictures in my brain, but the veil—the blue bikini—remains; a subtle quiver.

We were going home on the train, and it was night, when Ruth and I finally had a chance to touch. If you can make love to a hand, we did it. It was all we could do, sit there and fondle hands, my left hand and her right hand. The electricity we generated went through the heavens. The yearning for more, just holding hands, was an awakening of primordial eros. I fell in eros. And my relationship with Jesus was challenged, so determined was I to have a relationship with this unattainable... she wasn't a girl but a mysterious force. We both felt destined for each other, though we belonged to other people. She was "Tea Shop," and I was "Bible Club."

Consumed by desire for Ruth I took my argument to The Lord and poured out my anguish in my journal. It must have been blasphemous; I would later cut those pages out. Cut them out!? I have never cut or thrown my writing away. Now, I'd love to read what I wrote then. At any rate, Jesus won the battle, so I informed Ruth: "Before we can have a relationship, you must repent and ask Jesus into your heart." I was really surprised one night at the Friday night dance. I had come down from my dorm room and waited for her outside. She came out and I presented her with my ultimatum: Accept Jesus or it's over. I was shocked when she agreed, said the sinner's prayer and asked Jesus to come into her heart! What a sweet victory! But short-lived. Ruth left for the States just days later and missed the whole of grade twelve, while I spent the entire year in a daze of love letters. Every day after school, I ran up to Edge Hill mission house, where her letters arrived. There is nothing like the anticipation of a love letter, the abyss of an empty mailbox.

6

Bible College: Porn and Horror

Graduation day at Woodstock School should have been a time for weeping; weeping because I'd never see such friends again. I hadn't thought much about the fact that I wouldn't be living in India. I would live in another country, by myself. And it wasn't the time for mourning the loss of my childhood in India yet. In a day or two, our tight group of classmates would splinter to every corner of the globe. However, I was so eager to see Ruth, in Berne, Indiana, that I almost missed the crying and mourning.

It was tradition to have a "Wailing Line," which gave everyone a chance to say goodbye to the departing seniors. It was impossible not to cry. We were all crying, laughing, screaming, talking loud. Then we spent the rest of the night roaming the hillside, without a curfew, seeking connections with our closest mates.

And the next thing I knew I was in Indiana, at a house where Ruth lived with her parents and three younger brothers. I was entranced by the drift of big snowflakes, looking out the big front living room window. Her Dad was the pastor of "the biggest Mennonite church in the world." So I heard. After a few days we went together up to Michigan to be counselors at Camp Friedenswald, a Mennonite camp deep in the Michigan woods.

It was exciting to see Ruth. We did make out a lot, and I wanted to explore sexual boundaries that I had never crossed before. But I was having my first culture shock. After twelve years in school, seeing the same people, year in and year out, I found myself surrounded by new faces all the time... and so many pretty females I had never seen before. So I was soon smitten by someone other than Ruth, and abandoned her just as I had Bonnie. My guilt (for leaving Rachel, like Bonnie) was impotent against the new desire. It was a summer fling, and we managed to remain Christian virgins, though I knelt at her bed in the night.

****

While I was somewhat familiar with my loneliness, living in a small room in a rooming house, and working shifts in a factory, introduced me to a whole new level of my human condition. I felt not only alone but alienated from a sense of meaning.

My parents stayed in touch with the couple who had housed David five years earlier. One of the first things the lady said to me was an order: "Don't talk about India." What was there to talk about? Anyway, I got my first real summer job in a factory making cabinets. I would stand in my cubicle, gluing and stapling boards, feeling abandoned in the world, a stranger to everything and everyone around me. I would wonder to myself, how do other people experience this? The assault on my sense of senselessness felt cosmic in its depth. I wondered how people in the world could bear such a lonely feeling, if not die of sorrow. And now I missed my friends more than anything. I loved them all—hating the play-less oppressive world of sameness around me; the people I saw seemed superficial and characterless. I couldn't see them. The color that (just) is India, gone—Canada seemed the same in all directions.

****

Ontario Bible College was located, at the time, at Bloor and Spadina, a short subway to Yonge St, and endless porn shops. The college dorm itself was an old rooming house, destined to be torn down the following year. We assisted in the demolition with epic water fights, heaving industrial-size garbage barrels of water over the top banisters. We soaked each other's rooms.

The dorm house on Spadina was an easy walk to lots of greasy spoon restaurants, and a Young Mens Hebrew Association, where we lifted weights and played basketball, and where I sprained my ankle and had to wear a cast.

Toronto turns into brown slush in the winter. I think I had a desk by a window overlooking Spadina Avenue, across the street from the OBC library. I was sitting there one night, studying The Bible, of course, when my brother burst in, passing through on one of his adventures crisscrossing North America. He said he'd hitchhiked through every State three times over. He would regale people in bars, for beer and money, sharing war stories from Vietnam, and growing up in India. He reminded me of Tarzan more than anyone.

But he'd come to tell me about "what really happened to Mom." He corrected, brutally, my childhood version of "Mom's accident." "She didn't fall; Dad pushed her over a cliff, went down and smashed her head with a rock, and left her for dead!" I don't know if I was shocked, but I never spoke about it again until finally, six or seven years later, I asked Mom to tell me the story. That conversation would feed the perfect storm for my downfall as a missionary. But as a first year Bible College student, there was nothing to talk about; I didn't tell anyone. Jesus forgives everything, and I'd seen Dad's tears.

****

When I look back on my five years at The Ontario Bible College, what stays with me is the naive simplicity of the Evangelical approach. We took everything the Bible said at face value. I don't think we really cared about authorship; well, except for Moses and David, and all the prophets, and Mathew, Mark, Luke, and John, and St. Paul wrote the rest of them, though I recall some ambiguity over the book of Hebrews—a brilliant summation of Pauline Christology. John wrote Revelations, and Peter wrote his own books. We believed that we held the Closed Cannon Of Holy Scripture in our hands.

We read The Bible as a personal revelation. As Evangelicals, we understood how The King James version of the Bible was written in the vernacular of the people, of that time, *just as* The New American Standard Bible is now written in English, so everyone today can understand. We don't say thou, we say you. I became a follower of Tindale and the Bible Translators. Humans have the right to read The Bible in their own time and language.

The Bible was a magical book, though we'd never call it that. All I had to do was read, and let The Spirit teach me. The Bible was to be memorized and put into practice. We were called, as individuals, to devour the word—really eat it, think about it all the time, let it inform every activity of life. There was no need to question the Biblical text for historical context or inter-textual inconsistency. Each book and each verse had its own message and bore a connection to all the other verses of The Bible. The Bible was like one body, from cover to cover.

****

My favorite teacher, suspiciously Armenian, thought "works" were important evidence of salvation. He was not a Calvinist, as the rest of the faculty and most of the student body were. At any rate, he had a great British accent, and he enthused us to use our imaginations when reading The Bible. So I took his course on the book of Genesis. I think we were all embarrassed when he asked us to imagine what Adam must have seen, and what he felt, the first time he actually saw Eve—naked, parting the bushes and walking toward him. He wanted us to embellish that scene in our imaginations. I won't give you all the iterations of my own fantasy, but I have gone to some lengths trying to imagine the scene of The Fall—what really happened in East Africa eighty to ninety thousand years ago? (See Appendix #1)

****

We took evil and the devil seriously, and I have an experience to prove it. I fully believed that the devil (somehow) was taunting me from around every corner. It haunted me for months, and gave me sympathy for the problem humans can have with their minds. Mental problems are tormenting, because they never go away—they last forever—as long as you think so. Do you want hell? Have some more! I became a nervous wreck.

My roommate and I had done something we knew would never have been permitted, should we have asked. At the time I didn't know how Roman Catholic our behavior was: "It is easier to get forgiveness than permission." We went to see The Exorcist. The place was packed. Eventually, people were screaming and even vomiting in their seats. I was transfixed and drawn in by the collective state of nervous energy. I've never experienced anything like it. When the movie ended, however, that nervous hook stayed with me for days, for weeks, for at least a month, like a cramped muscle that wouldn't let go.

I remember because I was on the choir tour, which ended our semester before the summer break, and "the summer job." I thought all the singing would drive the devil away. During my free time, I memorized First John. The anxiety and the tension would not relent. I couldn't stop imagining the devil as a present reality, stalking me and ready to pounce from behind every corner. I didn't know how, I just felt it. When the choir disbanded, and we all went our separate ways, I found a place to live in the attic of a huge Presbyterian Church. I had a job chroming seat-belt parts at the General Motors Plant.

When I worked the afternoon shift, I'd have to walk into the Church in the dark. Then I had to climb the creaking stairs to the attic. The space inside the Church was dark and cavernous, and felt as alive as a monster breathing. One night, as I walked into my room and closed the door, the pulldown blinds fluttered open with a loud crack. I yelled out, terrified—this was it! The Devil had finally got to me! It was such a catharsis of fear, so much so, ironically, that the hook on my nervous system let go! The situation, the timing, was actually too funny to be taken seriously. Who knows about the devil, but that moment was too much like the punch line for a joke on me. And I knew it, but I still felt angry! The timing was too perfect; me sneaking successfully into my room after making it through the dark bowels of the Church, I flipped on the lights—the devil! But a harmless trick, after all, and worth a good laugh in the retelling.

****

Back to Bible College: On Friday nights, I would head down Yonge Street with a sack of gospel tracts, handing them out to people on the street. I joined the Hare Krishna's, The Children of God (COG), and a few other cult pushers with their propaganda, including the guys handing out porn shop flyers. They liked to show me how to be assertive in the way I handed out my tracts. They'd take a stack of my tracts and really get in people]s faces: here, take this, this is for you! You know you need it; you know you need Jesus! I know they were making mockery, but still I admired their fearless attitude.

I could not resist the porn shops. From the very beginning

of my journey into porn, I was always repulsed by the violence against women. It never made sense to me, and I would walk out (like Dad would've) when the themes never changed. I really was not turned on by what seemed like so much frightening male sexual aggression. I thought sex should look like the best fun, not like you are hurting someone! It was even too much for Jonny, who told me he wouldn't stand up for this—get outta here! But maybe pornography is just meaningless sex, and I was hooked. As Dad said, once you go down that road... "You'll end up drunk in an alley by the porn store."

****

Toward the end of my five years at The Ontario Bible College, I began a deep study of "The End Times." I devoured everything Hal Lindsey had written, and had been reading him already in the mid-70s and on. Like my grandfather before me, I became obsessed with the nature of unfolding events, to be seen in the world through the Biblical lens.

Everything about the Evangelical view of The End Times centers on what happens in Israel. Surprisingly, it was my mother who impressed this fixation with Israel upon me. She seldom instructed me directly about spiritual things. That was Dad's job. But I remember on two occasions, when as she talked, she gestured with an urgency that told me, "Take this personally, and do not doubt what I'm about to tell you... Never be distracted by The News; the only important thing in our world is what happens in Israel!" But on another time, and with equal passion, even taking my cheeks in her hands, she said, rather sternly, "Ted, you don't understand money, and you never will." Perhaps she was only reminding me of my middle name, Leavitt, the messengers who were never worried for provision.

Most people can't fathom the significance of the date, May 14, 1948. The establishing of Israel was not just another country being formed; this was God's will being done before our eyes, the very fulfillment of all the prophecies, the very direction of human history—Biblical History—being demonstrated before all eyes. The establishment of Israel was confirmation of our faith, and prophecy. The world would begin to see the truth of The Bible, and now Jesus could return for sure. It was just a question of figuring out some timelines, and plugging in the important characters.

The End Times centers on the actions of three main characters. These men must play their roles—before the return of Jesus. First, there must be an Antichrist. Then, there's a False Prophet who underlies and promotes the whole process. And finally, there has to be a Lawless Man, a brief and terrible time before Jesus returns to deal with the mess. I came to understand the system of The Antichrist as some sort of barcode military machine—guided by a repulsive image—raining fire from the skies on the people of Earth. The deception attributed to The Antichrist would be recognized as an individual who would utterly seduce the Christian world with his own seductive preaching, and, furthermore, systematically transform the global economy in support of his cause. His name would amount to 666. The False Prophet would be a writer who would develop an entire system of thought consistent with The Antichrist point of view, informing both The Antichrist and The Lawless Man.

When I was in Bible College in the early 70's, I was expecting to see the imminent rise of this whole Antichrist system—in Europe—and that America was just a country (an "Island country" the prophets had mentioned) that would come to the support of Israel.

After Bible College, I slowly gave up my fascination with end time prophecy and even began wondering about other Christian traditions. For a year I assigned myself the task of reading through everything CS Lewis wrote. So I didn't pay much attention to Ronald Reagan. And it wasn't until George

Bush became president (and I was no longer a practicing Christian) that I was one day flipping through the TV channels and came across The Hal Lindsey Report—a man I hadn't thought of in twenty years. A chill ran through me, a little horrifying, and an exhilarating recognition. The Evangelical world listens to Hal Lindsey—for all things "end times." Now I saw a very funny and tragic joke—laughing in my Evangelical face. From the Evangelical point of view, Ronald Reagan perfectly fulfills all the expectations of the Evangelical Antichrist. And Hal Lindsey, who called Obama The Lawless Man, is stuck with Donald Trump as The One who comes to clean up the mess made by his predecessors. Or maybe Hal Lindsey was wrong about Obama. I mean, I was wrong about Bush, who I thought was The Lawless Man.

****

But I had not yet graduated from Bible College, and I needed a wife. In order to continue in the calling I believed God had placed on me: a fantasy of taking the Gospel even further into darkness than my ancestors had gone, I'd become obsessed with the thought of evangelizing the Pashtuns of Pakistan. For this I would need a wife.

How I met my wife was a perfect demonstration of, "Ask, and you shall receive." During my evening devotions, I found myself making a list of criteria for my "wife to be." The next day, at lunch-time in the cafeteria, Lesly was sitting at a table with a number of other people. The conversation involved each person answering questions about themselves, and in the order of the items on my list! I had asked God to send me a missionary kid herself, someone who wanted to continue in mission work, specifically among the tribal people of the world. I also wanted a nurse, someone with Bible College training, and she had to discuss evidence of a devotional practice.

It hadn't occurred to me that she had to be attractive: if she met the crucial five requirements, who was I to deny the gift of God in answer to my prayers, no matter what she looked like. The first thing I noticed was how pretty she was. So I started asking my questions... where do you come from (missionary kid), what did you do before Bible College (nurse), what do you plan to do after Bible College (tribal mission work), what is your devotional practice (daily devotions). I got up from the table and walked, with my food tray, over to where my sister was already arranging dishes ,for a job we did together, in the school cafeteria. I marched up to her and announced: "See that woman over there? Her name is Lesly, and she's going to be my wife!" Joy was disbelieving at my presumptuousness, and laughed, "Nooo." But I was dumbfounded or smitten with conviction. I had asked, and God answered immediately. I followed.

7

Rough Beginnings

Enthralled by the conviction that Lesly would go out with me, I asked her on a date. A friend had already asked her out, and she had turned him down. "I'm not here to meet a man," she told him. He discouraged me when I mentioned my plan to ask her out. At any rate, what he said prepared me, so when I approached her, I had a little speech prepared. I said I wasn't interested in her merely as a girlfriend, that I was seeking a wife, and felt that she was the one for me, the answer to my prayers. She was interested, and we made a date. I think we went to a Dairy Queen. I became weirdly uncomfortable. We sat there and hardly talked. She said she was comfortable with silence; but I wanted to talk about everything. I wasn't sure she was interested in me in a way that I could recognize. I expected a lively conversation. After a few dates like that, I felt discouraged, trapped by the whole situation—I'd already committed myself to her. But Lesley was pretty, and her silence made me determined to probe beneath the surface. She seemed imperturbable.

Kissing helped patch over my lack of connection, and things got pretty hot. We sought counseling to find out how far we could go in our sex play. We wanted to be holy in the sight of God, and not sin. We knew that intercourse would constitute the sin of fornication (sex before marriage), but what about "petting"? Could we touch each other's genitals?

Could I fondle her breasts? We did our research, and even talked to a number of other engaged couples. We finally concluded that petting was OK, not a sin. It was the hottest sex we ever had. She could press against me and look down my pants. That was exciting enough for me.

The more trapped I felt by our engagement, however, the more I felt an uncontrollable awakening of sexual desire. I started talking on the phone with other women friends at the Bible College, and would masturbate quietly while we talked. I could be totally clandestine about it, and they never knew (as far as I know). I had found a whole new way of exploring the energy of lust. This behavior overwhelmed me and corresponded to the time of our engagement. It felt like sexual panic, trying to get away—but nowhere to go.

We had a very nice wedding, with all the appropriate bridesmaids and grooms, and a beautiful Evangelical ceremony. The night before, I found myself in a spiritual conundrum. As Evangelicals we are to eagerly await the second coming of Jesus, an event that can happen at any moment, and interrupt whatever's happening. But I was asking Jesus, please put off your second coming—for just one more night! I had waited twenty-one years for the moment, a moment when I would be forever relieved of the temptations of lust—because now my wife could satisfy me in any number of ways and at any time. I could hardly wait; but I felt shame, that my desire for my bride was clearly more vivid than any thought of Jesus and His return.

We'd been advised by a Christian counselor, not to get carried away on our honeymoon night. He thought the first night should be a time for experimentation—though he offered no suggestions. He left that up to our imaginations. If you have waited all your life to have sex with your wife, the chances are *that* first memory will get burned into your mind: so having sex with the crook of your new bride's knee will stay with you forever! I have no memory of the first time we had intercourse, but I remember the knee!

****

Before the honeymoon was over, I realized that my wife was, not nearly, as interested in sex as I was. This felt like a death sentence; I couldn't fathom it. Marriage is forever, and ever. Before the week was out I was making phone calls, this time to any single female in the Toronto phone book. I learned quickly: women hate and fear obscene phone callers. I didn't know it then, but I was part of the heyday for the official obscene phone caller. There was never a quicker cure for an addiction—to anonymous phone calls—than caller ID! Everything about the excitement depended on anonymity. It was a safe way for me to express my oppressed sexuality. But when I realized that I was scaring women, I was reminded of the violent porn I had seen on Yonge St. Were my phone calls a kind of rape? I was craving interesting conversation, though I was fixated on sex. I would have to be more seductive, minimize anxiety: become a real psychopath.

With practice, I could tell from the tone of voice whether a conversation could lead to connection. Lust is a vast energy web in the human aura. My phone-lust radar excluded men, children, and the elderly. I wanted a young, sexy female voice, one who knew better; someone lonely and sexually hungry. Emotionally mature women were not fooled. They invariably said the same thing, and cut through my trance, "You're behaving like a child, you have a problem and you know it." That would sober me, and I'd go back to the Bible and prayer. But this happened rarely, and the momentum of the addiction grew with determination and intensity. I could easily spend eight hours a day making phone calls. And, like gambling, it was reinforced by "intermittent reinforcement," the most powerful reinforcing pattern there is. You don't know when it's coming, but keep at it, because the reward is just around the corner. Someone will eventually talk with you, share their own sexual fantasies, and maybe even agree to meet. They might even take you back to their place. This happened at least a dozen times. But most often I would go to the agreed-upon place and wait. I got used to being stood up. Or, more likely, they did show but wouldn't approach me. Eventually, when the connection I was seeking didn't happen, there was the Yellow Pages with the "escort service" girls for a quick hand job. That was a last resort—it cost money, which bugged me.

****

Six months after the marriage I had sex with a stranger. It happened after watching the Super Bowl, the winter of 1979. The Cowboys, my favorite team, were playing. Watching football had become a passion during my five years at OBC. Too Tall Jones and Ed Newhouse thrilled me. I was a devoted Cowboys fan, and had watched every Super Bowl after moving to Canada in 1973. But on this particular evening, my wife determined that we had other social plans, which meant I would not be watching the Super Bowl. My wife didn't understand... Miss The Super Bowl Game?!—"Other plans?! Are you kidding me? You actually think I'm not going to watch the Super Bowl?" Well, she insisted, our social life superseded any kind of football game. I felt incorrigible; and decided, while she was at work, that I would disappear. I left the house for my old haunts on Yonge Street. Every bar had a television and The Game was on; I drank some beer and watched the game by myself.

After the game, I was drunk and in search of adventure, and I walked further down Yonge Street. The air was freezing and a light snow fell on the icy sidewalk. A woman walking in front of me suddenly, just like the movies, slipped and fell. I was right there, and with ease, helped her to her feet. Swept up in a mysterious and happy attraction; we blended our energies. We walked to the closest bar, had another drink, and then went to her place. She thought a miracle had taken place, having just moved, within days, from a small town in Manitoba. She was lonely in the big city. We spent the night together, and in the morning I told her I was married, and wouldn't be able to see her again. She was crushed and sad, and I felt miserable, a loss of self-worth.

When I finally got home, in the afternoon the next day, my wife was so glad to see me; I was really confused. She thought I'd died! She'd called the police and reported me as a missing person. She had fantasies of me "dead in a ditch somewhere"—not out with another woman! I broke down and confessed my sin and told her that I was still having sexual problems, and making phone calls. She forgave me, then, and would continue to forgive me. Until one day, fourteen years later, she'd think to herself, "Do I want to be doing this—fifty years from now?" No. She may well have saved us both. But we had only just begun a fourteen-year journey, very much centered on the issues of my sex addiction.

During the year, before going to Pakistan, I worked in a factory—making, packing, and shipping fire retardant insulation. Stuff you blow into walls. I'd get up at 4:30 AM for my devotions, then get on the first bus to the train, then a second bus to the factory. One of my jobs was to climb a veritable mountain of old newspapers and magazines, and toss, or hurl them down a shoot for thrashing. The shreds were then soaked in fire retardant chemistry. Then it was tested and compressed into bundles and finally loaded on a train car. I worked my way through all the different positions. The guys who worked there were hard-living pornographers. Porn pin-ups plastered the walls; they cursed for my education, and had no time for my evangelism. However, a Jamaican Rasta guy found my evangelical style funny. He drove me to the train after work, a marijuana-scented leaf hanging from his rear view mirror.

****

With the year of hard labor over, my wife and I flew to Delhi, where we joined other new missionaries with The Bible And Medical Missionary Fellowship. I had the feeling of being the star I was destined to be, for Jesus, my parents, and all my ancestors. The famous Garrison name would continue, and now be further recognized. I became a guide for new missionaries experiencing India for the first time. But inside, something else was going on; I was a mess.

After the new missionary training conference, we were able to take a short holiday and traveled with my parents up to Mussoorie, and Woodstock School. Back at the old school, I also returned as a star. The little kids remembered me, those basketball swish shots from the left side, the rebounds. But my wife became a stranger to me, like she didn't belong there. Somehow I knew that my own feelings for her were deeply unfair. I kept them to myself and could not understand them.

It was during this vacation when I finally asked Mom to tell me the truth about what happened with Dad. At that time, I also met with the missionary who'd been part of the rescue. He emphasized it as a miracle, that he alone could hear her call for help.

Following the conference and time spent with my parents, we crossed the border into Pakistan from The Golden Temple in the Punjab. We traveled in one of those vans that go everywhere, throughout the country, but only when filled with enough passengers. You wait a lot, and people look around. A lot of dealing seemed to be going on. A bad feeling crept over me. Pakistan, it turned out, was not at all like another Indian State. The eyes that looked at me were not what I saw in India, and expected to find, as well, in Pakistan. People in India, as a rule, didn't look at me with a glint of suspicion. But I felt it right away in Pakistan: I was not welcome. It scared me, and I wanted to get back to India, where I felt safe, and people were always friendly. Now I was experiencing what it would feel like to be a missionary in Pakistan. A nervousness crept over me.

Yet I really enjoyed the summer, learning to write and speak Urdu. I found the script easy and a joy to write. I remember how I struggled to learn Hindi in the class I took at Woodstock in high school. My teacher was discombobulated with me because, of all the white kids, I had the best Hindi pronunciation. Why was I so reluctant to speak? "Out with it, you can speak this," she'd say! But something in me had shut down. After speaking Gujarati as a child, then dabbling in Marathi in grade school (both languages my dad spoke fluently), and then Hindustani in North India—everything turned to "kitchardi" (mixed spicy salad) in my mind. So I quit trying to speak it; though I could understand a lot, I would still respond in English. At any rate, I enjoyed making headway in Urdu. Our Urdu teacher was a Muslim, with a flair for the stern style. If your pronunciation was wrong, he would say, "No, I disagree with you!" Waving his index finger then spiraling it up into the air. He said this so often I can still hear it, and use it in moments of playful correction.

****

But I had another problem with Pakistan. Pornography was not available, as far as I could tell. And I had no access to a private phone. I felt desperate. One day, when I was alone, I found myself opening the bedroom window in the hope that the cowherd girl might see me and get excited. But before she could notice, I thought to myself, wait a minute, this is a good way to get myself killed. What would the Muslims, already resenting the presence of missionaries, do with someone like me? I didn't want to find out. But I felt powerless over what I was doing.

We returned to Delhi for a second round of new missionary training. I took them on a tour through The Red Fort, Agra, and the Taj Mahal. In Delhi, there was a phone in the mission headquarters, and I tried to make some anonymous calls. I was surprised to find I could, and made a couple of connections on the phone with friendly female voices. But then I thought, surely the Indian government has bugged these phones, keeping track of what the missionaries are saying in secret. That made me paranoid, which totally interrupted my sense of freedom to make calls. I do find the prospect of "getting caught" a real deterrent. Then I found myself climbing outside the mission building to see if I could peek into the bathroom, or bedroom windows, of other young female missionaries, or couples. Maybe I could actually see them having sex. It didn't happen. This desperate and fruitless act felt like a last straw. There was no one I could talk to. And I was respected as someone who would not have such awful problems. What was I doing?!

In a state of "flight panic"(I don't know what else to call it), one day, while the other missionaries were out, (I made some excuse not to participate), and with a pile of Indian rupees, got a taxi and went to the Delhi airport. I would return to Pakistan, fill a back pack, access our bank account, and buy a plane ticket to Amsterdam and Times Square. I felt a resolute determination to get away—before I did something that might get me killed, and humiliate everyone. When I reached the airport in Delhi, they told me, "No American can purchase a plane ticket with rupees." I joked around with them, to seem as local as could be, speaking some Hindi. They gave me a ticket! God or the devil was on my side. The first miracle. When I arrived in Islamabad, I asked our travel consultant to get me on a plane out of the country—that evening. He said, "That's impossible."

I said, "I'm heading up to Murree and I'll return later in the day for the ticket." He was doubtful, but I didn't care; I was determined to leave. Back at the mission bungalow in Murree, the missionary resident there was shocked and confused, and though I said nothing, she sensed something was wrong. She suggested I talk with Bob Morris, the director of the Mission, who would be "coming by shortly." Without responding, I threw a few things in my backpack and charged back down the hill in the same taxi. Apparently, I missed Bob by fifteen minutes. If I had waited, I'm sure he could have talked me out of my escape-trance. Bob had been my chief Christian influence through Woodstock and Bible College.

I had asked the travel consultant to arrange my trip through Amsterdam, but there wasn't enough money in our account for that. All he could do was get me to Karachi, and from there, on the most direct route, to New York. I was disappointed; how I wanted to see the famous sex shops in Amsterdam. NY would have to do.

In the hotel that night, in Islamabad, I had another fling with madness. Crawling naked out of my window, I climbed precariously across a very narrow ledge, of just an inch or two, to see if I could peek into the next bathroom window. It was a very dangerous thing to do, in many ways. There was no footing or hand grips in case of a fall. I've often wondered what anyone looking up from the street, ten floors below, might have seen. A naked white guy climbing on the outside of the building?! Why? It gives me the chills.

On the plane the next day, from Islamabad to Karachi, I had my first (and hopefully last!) brush with suicidal thoughts. Heading into Karachi the plane went into a terrible storm. The pilot had to veer up from the runway—twice—before he could safely land. As the tension and fear of the people around me grew, reacting to the battering winds and vain attempts to land, I felt an eagerness for the plane to crash—smash into smithereens! It felt absolutely appropriate. And all the people on the plane wouldn't know: this was my punishment—for me leaving the mission field on a mad quest for some pornography, an abysmal failure! My life, as I knew it, was over—and I knew it! My eagerness for death felt strangely empowering. The plane landed safely, and I felt more bound than ever in my quest for some pornography.

51

****

I was heading for New York and looking forward to all the sex in the world. As soon as the flight from Karachi landed in New York, I went straight down to 42nd Street and into one of those spacious places, completely devoted to porn, with rooms in the back for who knows what. Passing large tables covered in disheveled mounds of random fleshy magazines, I went to the back and into a booth that required 75 cents to lift a veil. What could be on the other side? There were three skinny young women, two of them lying back and masturbating on low rotating tables. A third woman walked promptly over to my open window and stood there naked—right in front of my face, looking down to see what I'd do with Jonny. Oh yeah, Jonny. Remember Jonny, Ted! Jonny!—this is what we came all this way for! But the emotional weight of my situation was crashing down on me. I'd come all the way from Pakistan—for this! This was the time for an erection—and someone's watching!

Nothing, nada, just a numb emptiness—not a hint of excitement. Turning around, I walked back outside to 42nd Street and into the brilliant New York sunshine. Leaning against a wall, standing in the sun, the full impact of what I'd done was sinking in. I knew I was facing a life-changing event, but I had yet to find out just how. The pornography felt empty and pointless, and I hadn't even tried to masturbate. Now there was nothing in New York that I wanted. The fantasy had burst. Standing there in the sun, it struck me how alone I really was, because no one (in the whole world) knew where I was. That was a first. I wasn't in Pakistan, or India, or Canada. And no one would have imagined me on 42nd St. in New York. I had failed in my missionary calling... and felt the accusing gaze of my missionary ancestors, as far back as The Mayflower, and who knows how much further back, maybe all the way to St. Thomas! But most of all, I was a failure in the sight of The Lord. My sense of a meaningful life was in smithereens; as though the plane had really crashed.

With no plan, I stayed in a hotel, bordering Central Park, and drank Heineken beer for the first time. Then I went up to my room and made some fruitless phone calls. When morning came, I realized that I had to "face the music." I had to call the Director of the Mission and say something—but what? That I could no longer be a missionary. But I couldn't tell him why. He wanted to see me in Toronto asap.

The director of our mission was a big Italian man, renowned for his preaching. He inspired me. However, when I walked into his office, what he said almost made me laugh out loud. "You sit on that chair and crap like a man!" It was as though he tried to "scare the shit out of me"—but I had instant constipation. I couldn't tell him anything, but said that I would talk with someone else—like a therapist. That just made him angry, so he began guessing at what my problem was, as though maybe, if he just said the worst thing, it would loosen my tongue. "What's your problem?" he asked angrily. "Are you a homosexual? Don't you know your wife can help you with your problem?" He actually said that. That didn't help me talk; though it seemed like a reasonable "Hail Mary," given the circumstances.

What could be a worse sin than homosexuality? An obscene phone caller? I said, "No sir, that's not my problem, but I still won't talk with you about it."

"Fine," he said, "then I know someone who helps us with the psychological evaluation of new missionaries. You'll have to talk with him." So he made an appointment for the next day.

It was a brief and memorable initial interview. I don't remember what I told him, but at some point, he said, "This is what we're going to do. You have two hours to make a decision: whether you'll return to Pakistan, and get some help there, or stay here and get some help; but either way you need counseling. Come right back here in two hours and tell me what you want to do."

Walking from the therapist's office, I wandered aimlessly down the street. I looked at the tall buildings, the shiny glass windows, the cars and shops, all clean and tidy and civilized, not like downtown New York, and forever away from Pakistan. I came upon a tiny little city park with a bench surrounded by a small patch of grass. I was alone and it was another sunny day.

What surprised me, honestly, was how completely uncertain I felt. I felt open, excited, and dreadful at the same time. But with no idea what to do, or how to decide. Go back, or stay?? Still, I tried to think through the issues, struggling for clarity. No clarity came. If I went back to Pakistan... could I just pick up where I left off? But did I really want to go back? On the other hand, if I stayed in Canada, I would face a completely uncertain future—and would have to find a new reason to live. When my entire life was devoted to being a missionary, what could I do now? I couldn't decide. It felt really strange to (almost) relish in my helpless uncertainty. But I had to decide, and the minutes were ticking away. This was no time for luxuriating in not knowing.

Well, then, I thought, if nothing was clear, I might be forgiven for resorting to a forbidden, magical practice: open the Bible randomly, and with the eyes closed, point to a verse and accept it as guidance. I had a light blue colored New American Standard New Testament in my back pocket, which I always carried with me for memorization practice. The cover was worn and wrapped in shredding plastic. Having decided the method for making my decision, I sat there quietly, not daring to pray... for the shame of stooping to such a questionable procedure. But I was desperate and could think of no other way to find the guidance I really needed. Opening the New Testament, I pointed to a verse and got the story of Jesus speaking to Peter: "You will not be able to follow me now, but I have prayed for you, and after you have been tested, you will follow." Wow!—that seemed pretty clear! But I was still doubtful. I thought, given the circumstances, that I had a right to be completely certain—no magic, a real miracle! If God could speak once, that clearly, He could do it again. Opening my little New Testament again, I pointed and got the verse where St. Paul is speaking about his companion Barnabas flunking out on the missionary tour with him! That was enough. I couldn't believe it. To have received such startlingly clear guidance made me feel insanely happy! Maybe God can use magic! It was obvious I would stay in Canada and get the help I needed.

Walking back to the therapist's office, within the allotted time, I told him what had happened. Maybe he could help.

****

Meanwhile, my wife stayed with my parents in India for a whole month. I can't imagine the depth of feeling between her and my parents. I began getting individual therapy while waiting for her return to Canada. The therapist used Transactional Analysis. It's the kind of therapy where you teach people therapy as part of the process. I was hooked—analyze me! He seemed like an intelligent man, and not dogmatic in his faith, which we never discussed. He got me interested in trying to understand my problems, and in learning to be as honest as I could about them.

I met my wife at the airport and felt a heartbreaking love for her as she walked toward me in a long beautiful rust colored Indian style dress. She looked so pretty and sweet and innocent. I could tell she had cried a lot, and I longed to measure up to her accepting and forgiving spirit. But it was not to be.

We moved in with her parents, who lived in Kitchener/ Waterloo, Ontario, and stayed there for about a year. I felt stuck, in a numb state, without any idea what to do with my life; although, I knew I wanted to do something ordinary. For a while I became a Fuller Brush salesman, but I could not convince people that they really needed anything I had to sell. Fuller Brush did have a popular Bissell that worked well on most carpets, but not the shaggy kind—as I found out. That's a funny memory. I'd show people (once they let me in) how the Bissell worked: crunch up some cracker crumbs and throw them down on the carpet, then impress them with how well the Bissell did in picking up the mess. Once, I threw the crumbs down on a more shaggy carpet, and the thing just jammed as soon as I tried. The lady grinned evilly at me. Even while I was crunching up the crackers, I could tell by her expression that something was up. Realizing she had a vacuum cleaner that would clean up the crumbs, she took her time watching me embarrass myself, trying to get the thing to work.

But I wanted a more manly job. I would get my professional truck driving license! Be a man—drive a truck! It took me a month of training to get a license to drive the 18-wheelers. Four or five fellow trainees were hunched up in the back bench at 6 AM, while the trainer sat in the passenger seat where he could control the brakes if he needed to. I really enjoyed learning how to back a long truck down a narrow alleyway without hitting the sides.

But I couldn't get a job as a truck driver, and I had no experience to show for it. The only time I actually made use of it was to help my wife's sister with a move. She needed a big truck and someone with a truck driver's license. After unloading her stuff, I drove back in the empty truck, and while pulling away from a gas station noticed a hitchhiker with enormous breasts and blonde hair. It looked as though she could fulfill all my fantasies. And sure enough, as soon as she got in the cab she offered to give me a hand job for twenty bucks, and I could even touch her breasts if I wanted. I had the money and was eager. But then I made the mistake of asking her, "First, tell me a little about your life." It turned out she had a sad story, and was now a single mom trying hard to make ends meet. She had a phone bill and rent to pay, and the landlord was threatening to throw her out if she didn't come up with the cash immediately. Then I felt so heartbroken and tender toward her my lust evaporated. All I could say was, "I'd like to give you the twenty dollars, but I can't do the sex thing with you now." She flared up angrily and didn't want the money, demanding that I let her out right there on the side of the road. But the experience got me thinking. I had thought lust was the most overriding energy in the world. Yet lust seemed to require a kind of objectification that overlooked feelings of tenderness and care. Maybe my experience of lust required a deeper analysis. Maybe I could study it, and find out why it had such a grip on me.

****

The University of Waterloo offered correspondence courses in Psychology. Would studying psychology help me to understand myself better? I was at a new threshold in my wrestling with God. For a few days, I struggled with the idea of studying psychology. Would I be admitting that my love for Jesus and the Scriptures was not healing me from lust? I felt hopeless when I thought about buckling down to yet more Bible study, prayer, and memorization. My interest was turning inexorably toward psychology. And besides, I would only take a correspondence course, just to see if I was interested. So I signed up for two courses that seemed relevant to me: Psychopathology and Early Childhood Development. It was the psychopathology course that really got my attention, and inspired me to actually attend classes at the University of Waterloo. My brain felt charged by new ideas and ways of thinking. For the first time in my life I felt as though I was beginning to think for myself, and about a subject that threatened to become more interesting to me than the Bible.

My wife was able to work as a nurse, and was making enough money for us to move into a place of our own, and even helped pay for my classes. I needed hope for myself, and an explanation for my problems... and maybe, then, even help other people with their problems! I was a model of "the wounded healer." As I grew to know the other psychology majors, it began to dawn on me that most of us were especially troubled human beings. Why did the kids studying engineering seem so normal? But I wanted to know: what is the connection between childhood trauma and problems in adult life?

****

As we settled into our marriage, and felt some basic stability, we began to consider the possibility of having a child. Now, I don't know what other parents experience when they conceive a child, but my wife and I knew it when it happened—with both of our children. My wife had stopped using an IUD. I don't know how long after that it was, but the orgasm, for both of us, felt like an ocean wave, and we both burst into tears!—not suspecting that we had conceived a child. We had never experienced such a wave of oceanic love... When it happened again a year later, when our daughter was conceived, we understood, right away, that we had experienced another miracle.

We named our first child Nathan. My favorite story in the whole Bible, or the most interesting and strange, (besides Jesus, of course), was the King David and Bathsheba story. That story made the Bible very real to me. It's the kind of experience that real human beings have, full of seduction, conniving, sex and murder. You couldn't make up a story like that; it had to have actually happened. In the end, when the prophet Nathan is told by God to confront the King, he tells the king a story, as though it were an actual occurrence in his neighborhood, and the prophet was seeking some advice from the king. A very rich guy, with lots of resources, and sheep to spare, was having a feast and needed a sheep for the dinner. So he asks his servant to go out and take the neighbor's only sheep and slaughter it for the king's dinner party. Then Nathan asks the king, "What shall we do with that man?" And King David says, "He should be punished severely, and here's how..." Then the prophet Nathan points straight at King David and says, "Thou art the man."

Spiritual Exercises

During my last semester, studying for a BA in Psychology at the University of Waterloo, I took a class at St. Jerome College called "Christian Mysticism and Spirituality." What an eye opener for me: an MK, Bible College, the trajectory from St. Paul to St Irenaeus Luther to Billy Graham. University education challenged my narrow version of the Jesus story. That little crack eventually lead me to secular historians who honestly doubt the historicity of Jesus, suggesting that the Jesus event developed from a synthesis of deep myth and access to political power. My research would go on for years—but I was left with just another mystery: how did someone, who may not have existed, become the Jesus we are generally familiar with? I think that's astonishing! I do think the Jesus story/ myth has universal significance and gets at the problem, the remedy for human re-sentiment. But, hidden behind a narrative, the Roman genius for religious synthesis had something to do with bringing us the Image of Jesus, the Emperor: King Jesus of "The Family," and The Insurrection.

I remember the way my Church History professor at Bible College chuckled over his description of The Desert Fathers. He was a tall guy with a deep, resonant voice. "Imagine Simon the Stylite... a man who went out to the desert, climbed a thirty-foot tower of rock, and stayed up there for thirty years... chuckle... this is not a good example of what our Lord Jesus would expect of us. We can safely skip over such reactionaries and make our way straight to Martin Luther and John Calvin." I wrote a fifty-page essay on Martin Luther, the gnarly champion of my personal faith: "A mighty fortress is our God, a bulwark never failing... though still our ancient foe doth seek to work us woe, his craft and power are great, and armed with cruel hate, on earth is not his equal..."

The class at St. Jerome College introduced me to St. Anthony of The Desert and writers of The Philokalia. I read Meister Eckhart and the Rhineland mystics. These writers provoked a more psychological spirituality, so foreign to my virginal Evangelical ears. The Desert Fathers used a language of personal struggle, and they were honest about their inner experience.

And then I read Thomas Merton's "New Seeds of Contemplation." Merton, himself a convert to the Roman Catholic Church, had become a reclusive Carmelite monk. He wrote a lot. His book was a direct challenge to my Evangelicalism. After reading his book for the third time, I felt my tether to the Evangelical church come loose. I was sitting back on a lounge chair in the Student Union building. The ceiling was low above me and opened up toward the center, and daylight. I felt a seismic shift approaching, a distinctly physical sense of drifting from my Evangelical center of conviction, and a sort of thrilling dread—that I would never return. The sensation was that of a ship that's lost its moorings, a familiar image (I'm sure now) for so many in my situation. I sensed that I would, forever after, be prone to the uncertainty of meaning. Perhaps I would end up in a bad place, come to a faulty conclusion, and follow any number of paths—to nowhere.

A vague memory, or thought, came to me, that as a child, and as a Bible College student, I'd had this recurring sense, or fantasy: What would it be like to believe something other than what I believe now? I tried to imagine: could I possibly not believe in Jesus? Should I kill myself now, if I knew what I might become? What if I lost my relationship with Jesus? In fact, once, I played with this—by a kind of accident. I was in the Bible College library, sitting across from one of the new students. I happened to be reading Siddhartha by Hermann Hesse. I don't remember why I was reading that book, perhaps because I'd heard that Hesse was raised in India. The freshman gal asked me what I was reading, and why. So I played a game with her and myself. I said, "I'm actually a Buddhist, and I'm here to study Christianity." She believed me—which I came to realize as the conversation went on. I was trying to represent the Buddhist path as though I knew what I was talking about. What a dangerous experiment for any true believer! Concerned for her, and my growing vulnerability to the simple "be here now" of Buddhist teachings, I felt compelled to stop the ruse and bring the conversation back around to Jesus.

****

Irony is a funny thing, when looking back on it. Having completed my BA in psychology from UW, in spite of my love for Thomas Merton, I applied to the Christian and Missionary Alliance (C&MA) Seminary in Regina, Saskatchewan, and was accepted. My parents had been missionaries with the C&MA; the very mission that had thrown them out. Now I was on my way toward a Master of Divinity Degree under their guidance! In fact, the head of the mission, who was responsible for the decision to expel my parents, was preaching one Sunday in the local C&MA Church. I hadn't met the man, and had to introduce myself. "I'm the son of John and Leona Garrison, and I was born after my dad tried to kill my mom, as you know. And you have never spoken with them since that day, nor extended any kind of message of forgiveness. Why?" He didn't speak, and I was puzzled but not totally surprised. I felt all this baggage, heavy on me, and wanted to understand something, but he sat stoically and never said a word. In those days I was preoccupied with the thought: If Mom had not forgiven Dad... and had sex with him... I would not be here.

I had learned from the Seminary that I could major in Christian Counseling and Reality Therapy. I would be instructed and supervised by a trained RT therapist. He also taught another method: Deliverance Ministry. We began the semester listening to and discussing his recordings of "deliverance" sessions, where his team of therapists cast out demons.

The first three days at the Seminary, however, reminded me of being back in the furniture factory, or like crossing into Pakistan from India, that sinking feeling that I didn't belong. What differentiated this moment was the worst sort of boredom. More chapels, Bible talks, and prayer meetings. I couldn't take it. I had the sensation, growing every day, of having eaten way too many donuts. "Not another donut, please; I just ate a whole box." And then... I listened to the "deliverance sessions," and that was it, that sealed the matter. It sounded like a wild argument between an angry, scared, and sad woman and an angry man—yelling at a place in her that didn't want to speak. I thought to myself, just give me some basic psychology! I hadn't had enough of Freud, Jung, and Adler, for starters. I wanted Fritz Perls and Milton Erickson. How could I endure more of the same tired hymns, and "Dear Lord Jesus..." I walked out one day during a class break, following up on a whim to drive across town and check out the University of Regina.

In short order, I applied to their Masters in Clinical Psychology. They looked at my transcripts and said I would first need to take the "Honors in Psychology"—a year-long program. The Honors program involved a huge oral and written test at the end of the year. I was expected to pass the exam, and all the other class assignments. I did that, and passed the final exam with flying colors; but there was a problem: the Clinical Testing class.

The students were required to test the native children who lived in the Regina, with an intelligence test called the WISCR (Wechsler Intelligence Test for Children—Revised). We learned about the history of the test. It had been standardized on white kids in Iowa. The results of our tests were to be used by the Canadian government in their own research. Everything was going well until one day I was sent to the home of a Saskatchewan native kid who had been up all night with police in the house. The test indicated that he was "retarded" (teacher's words)—but I thought that was ridiculous. He was not a white midwestern kid, and he was living in a state of trauma. I cried in the class when I presented my results, suddenly angry about the whole testing business and how it was being used. I refused to surrender my results, if it meant that the data would actually be used in any significant way. I begged for another option: write an essay, do some research, whatever. No, I had to hand over my results. I wouldn't do it. They gave me a WF (withdrawal failure) for the class, which meant I had not completed the requirements for the Clinical program.

I didn't know, at the time, what a deliverance that was. I really wanted to study psychotherapy, not test people! What was I doing in a Clinical program—when there was another department, in Education, with a whole M.Ed. in Counseling Psychology?! It turned out to be a perfect fit, and I was even able to get some financial help, and office space as a Teaching Assistant. I had a lot of fun in that program, recording counseling sessions, being evaluated and evaluating other students. It became my goal to become a Licensed Professional Counselor.

****

It was during this time that I became interested in the concept of "Spiritual Direction" and met with a Jesuit Priest who agreed to guide me through The Spiritual Exercises of St. Ignatius. Father Monty kept me on the "first week" of the Exercises for a year. He kept confronting my stubborn preoccupation with Bible interpretation. He didn't want interpretation, he wanted my experience. He considered The Scriptures a familiar backdrop for viewing existential human drama. He would ask: "Well, were you bored during your meditation? What were you feeling at the time? I don't want to know what you thought of the passage, I've read the commentaries. I want to know what you experienced in your prayer time." I didn't get it. Had my Bible become a Rorschach Test for analyzing myself?

Along the way I had developed an enduring interest in dreams, and working with the dreams of clients. The study of dreams nourished my new sense of spirituality. The Bible, after all, is loaded with dreams and dream states. Dream study showed me a consistent practice for "looking within." I read everything I could on dreams and found a way to record them. To encourage dream recall, I learned how to turn back into the position I'd been in when the dream occurred. To prime my dreams, the night before, I noted the date in my notebook, placed on a desk level with the bed, and managed to write with my eyes closed. In the morning I just had to figure out the scrawl! I had a collection of 120 good books on dreams. Eventually I would facilitate an ongoing Dream Appreciation Group and teach numerous weekend workshops. I attended a huge conference on dreams at the University of Virginia. It became my basic way of motivating clients in the search for meaning, a way to explore their own path into the inner world. My active engagement with dreams and dreamwork went on for a good fifteen years.

Two dreams from that time have stayed with me, and continue to inspire me to look deeper for the meaning. I called the first dream "Abraham's other dream." In the dream, I'm walking down a street in Banff, Alberta. It's evening and the lights are on; the street is sparkling and packed with tourists in fancy dress. I'm directed suddenly to pick up a beautiful blonde child—a four-year-old—and kill her. The command comes through me as an unquestionable authority, inseparable from my own will, and I'm not aware of the slightest resistance within me. I don't question the command, and have no moral objection. I walk over to the child, pick her up and begin walking away from the crowds toward a dark and secluded area dotted with large boulders. As we walk, I become aware that the child and I have a deep bond, as though we have always known each other, and loved each other.

She relates to me as someone she trusts, like a father who she has no reason to fear. I am aware of this, and yet remain undeterred from what I have to do. As we reach an area, far enough away from the tourists and the lights, I take her by the heels and smash her head over a rock. This does not kill her, and I realize I must continue to finish her off. I take her in my arms again and feel her face. It's mangled; the bones are shattered, and her teeth are all misplaced. There's a lot of blood. Yet the little girl continues to relate to me just as she had before, with no sense whatsoever that I have done anything to cause her to fear me or to blame me. She doesn't act hurt.

Now this causes me to weep, but not to change my sense of unquestioning obedience to the command that I kill her. I walk over to a precipice with a waterfall and throw her over. Dispatched of my duty, I walk away. As I do so, I look across the street, where all the tourists are, and notice the same little girl in the arms of another man—unhurt—as though nothing has happened! For a brief moment, I'm stunned, and then wonder: now what will he do with the child? But I no longer feel responsible; I have followed the command to kill the child. I simply walk calmly away from the area.

In another dream (I call "the rose in the garbage"), I catch a glimpse of a young woman's face, glancing off a discarded cardboard box, and in the midst of some garbage men. What I see is a face that's sweet—alive—innocent. As in the previous dream, her face bears no judgment or fear or blame, and simply shines toward me through the heap of trash.

****

Then, our daughter was born. We named her Cara. From our research into names, I recall that Cara has the meaning of "a friend through bitter times." And indeed, I think my first conscious experience of unconditional love, extended to me, came from Cara when she was about eighteen months old. She'd caught pneumonia, and we realized we'd better take her to the emergency room. While holding her in my arms, a couple of nurses began trying to draw some blood, or place a needle into her arm for some reason. Anyway, it was not working, and I looked down to see this long needle going in and out in a futile attempt by the nurse to find a vein. They realized they needed to focus on their task, perhaps sensing my emotional turmoil. They asked if they could please take her from me into another area where they could place her on a steady table to perform the procedure. It seemed to take forever as I listened to her screams.

I stayed with her all night, sitting up in a chair across from her. She had settled down and was sleeping. Cara was an incorrigible thumb sucker, and there was nothing we could do to stop her. They had tied her arms down to prevent her from sucking her thumbs, as that would interfere with her breathing. At any rate, some time in the night she woke up briefly and searched the room with her eyes, obviously confused by the surroundings. And then glanced across the room and saw me, broke into a beaming smile and went straight back to sleep. Something happened in that brief glance that stays with me, like one of those "holy instants" A Course In Miracles talks about.

I was smitten by the innocence of love. I'd been feeling

like a moral failure. Despite having a stable outer life, nothing much had changed inside me. I was learning a lot and enjoying the study of psychology, but nothing was changing my compulsion to make phone calls. I was just getting better at it. And here I was with two beautiful kids, and about to earn a Masters in Counseling Psychology! I had clients. I was beginning to help other people with their own problems. But that sweet smile, in that moment, communicated something about absolute love that showed me how love is not bound to my own self concept: it just was—is. Love just is.

I knew in that moment that true love does not change, and is not based on the past or the future. There was nothing I could do to make love happen, it was something to know, or not, as a fact of being. It was as though I saw through her eyes to the innocence within me, that I'd forgotten in my shame. I would still have to learn how clinging to the language of sin makes forgiveness impossible. In that single brief glance I had tasted the perfection of a love that transcends time—but can be known in the now.

After graduating from the Masters in Counseling, I got a job as a "Youth Worker," which is "Canadian" for a probation officer working with teenagers. I was finally doing work I wanted to do, and that made some use of my education and interests. At the same time I was building a private practice, and, along with another woman therapist, developing the counseling program associated with the Second Baptist Church of Regina, where our little family was attending regularly.

****

Two steps forward and one step back. Or quite a few back. I don't remember what the last straw was for my wife, but she'd finally had enough of my chronic sexual acting out, and the confessions after the fact. And I couldn't have a real affair, though I came close with someone I'd met over the phone. She knew one of my professors at the University, and she knew that I was married. We met for a couple of weeks, secretly, but I couldn't take the strain of acting out on a long term basis. It was one thing to have sex on the phone, or meet someone for a "quicky," it was another thing to develop feelings for someone. I could not let myself fall in love with another woman. Divorce was not an option. I couldn't go on with the affair. When I confessed the affair to my wife, she requested a separation—"So you can do your thing, and I wouldn't have to hear your confessions."

She'd done everything she could to help me, even taking our big phone to work with her, so I couldn't use it! One of her fellow nurses wondered what in the world she was doing with the big phone in her bag. It was too embarrassing to talk about, and she had a hard time coming up with lame excuses. It didn't matter anyway, as I found a long extension cord and used the neighbor's phone; they always kept their doors open when they were away.

****

The separation felt like a liberation, initially. I had the sense that I could finally feed my sexual fantasies without limitations. I had met a couple of male friends who loved going to the bars, one who just loved to talk and argue psychology and philosophy. The other guy was a big Saskatchewan Indian, also studying psychology at the University. He seemed bright and mysterious and acted like he knew me. He disappeared later, for a year, and when he returned he said he'd signed up with American special forces to South America, and followed orders to kill people without question, attacking and terrorizing whole villages.

He claimed he was paid by rich oil barons from Texas. They gave him ten thousand dollars a month to follow orders and kill without asking questions. He didn't know who he was killing, or why, but thought he was making a lot of money. I didn't know what to believe. But he sure could pick up women. He wore jewelry and dressed fancy. I was always a wallflower. We made a strange couple of guys, and he encouraged me in my pickup strategies. He could tell when a woman was attracted to me—I had no idea. He loved the discos, and that's where I discovered that I might love to dance. But in those years I didn't go to the disco/bar to dance; I went to pick up women. I learned, that if I was just patient and stayed in a bar till closing time, there was always a very good chance I could meet a recently separated and lonely woman. At one point I was involved with eight women, and had a threesome going on with a couple in the neighborhood. It was all starting to feel emotionally complicated, meaningless, and actually unsatisfying.

****

I don't remember who gave me Pat Carnes' book called "Sex Addiction." I'd never heard that sex could become an addiction. I thought of lust as a spiritual problem, and the obsession with it, the result of childhood problems, and that therapy was required for treatment. Calling it an addiction seemed weird. But when I read the book, and the stories that went with it, I recognized myself. It read like a novel I couldn't put down, and I wanted to learn more about "sex addiction."

There were no sex addict type groups in Regina. Nobody had heard of it. As I began to research it, I first discovered a group in the United States called Sexaholics Anonymous. I found the phone number of the founder and called him. It was like talking with a long lost brother. He'd been a pastor, and still considered himself an Evangelical Christian. He did have a suggestion for what I had to do: admit I was powerless over lust, and start a twelve-step program, myself! He sponsored me until I could find some fellow "Sex Addicts" willing to use the twelve-step program. I became open about it and found a Community Center that would allow a free space for meetings. The community center staff were familiar with other twelve-step programs, and could find no objection to a room being used for yet another twelve-step meeting. I put a notice in the paper and started regular meetings. I even went out to the jail to talk with sex offenders. For months I was often the only person at the meeting. Then a local Catholic priest started coming. A couple of native Indian guys came, and a woman started coming regularly. One of the lessons I learned from that experience is that, if you really want something to happen, you must show up for three years—with the zeal of a religious commitment! Ten years later, I would go back to Regina to visit, when I was working with sex addicts as a therapist at a center in North Dakota, and found the room full—at least thirty people! It was a hero's welcome, and I felt satisfied to have persisted through the opposition from city officials.

The social workers and therapists in Regina could not imagine a twelve-step program for people with sexual compulsivity problems. Wouldn't it just make things worse—listening to other people talking about sex? Surely it would trigger our problems, not resolve them. And they wanted a professional to be present at our meetings—if they were going to support it. I flatly refused. There was no way in hell some therapist was going to be there, sitting in judgement. I tried to care less if they supported me or not. I knew that there were tons of ordinary people suffering from compulsive sexual behavior, and just needed to talk with other people about it without judgment or cross-talk. We needed to hear that we were not alone in our struggles. It is the emotional pain, we shared, that centered the group. We were not entertained by our stories—to act out more—we felt moved and compassionate for each other. I never once had the sense that anyone came for the entertainment. Only a non-sex addict would imagine a twelve-step meeting as an occasion for…drinking more, eating more, sexing more, gambling more... more religion.... We were in too much pain to consider our sharing as "entertainment." But yes, our twelve-step stories certainly are entertaining: the worse—the better!

****

I heard that Pat Carnes had founded a treatment center for sex addiction at The Golden Valley Health Center in St. Paul, Minnesota. I called them about the program, and they interviewed me to see if I qualified as a sex addict in need of treatment. They were hoping that I'd be a little more depressed and suicidal, and I reminded them about how I wanted the plane in Pakistan to crash, how I left the mission field and my wife for some porn on 42nd St. And I was having a lot of dreams about being shot. So they accepted me.

The program cost $25,000, and I didn't have that kind of money. The Canadian government, I discovered, would cover any kind of necessary treatment, in the US, if one could not find the treatment in Canada. Since there were no treatment centers for Sex Addiction in Canada (unsurprisingly), they agreed to pay for my treatment! Now that was a miracle. I was the second Canadian—and it turned out, the last—they would pay for such treatment. I told my immediate boss about my determination to attend the treatment center, and he was supportive. He promised, naively, to hold my job for me. When I did return, the "higher-ups" had informed him that the government was not prepared to tolerate (the concept of) a "sex addict" working as a probation officer. What if people found out? What would that do for the reputation of Social Services?

That first evening at the treatment center blew my mind. After dinner in the Hospital cafeteria, the patients (at least twenty of them) gathered in the main lounge. They were each given two minutes to share the story about what brought them to the treatment center. When my turn came, I couldn't speak for a while and just cried. It was the "coming home" experience: a place where I could share everything, without being overwhelmed by shame, judgment and misunderstanding. It was a place where I could begin to see how the patterns of childhood, especially forms of abuse, contribute in precise ways of acting out. Every form of sexual acting out, mirrored, in some way, exactly what had happened in childhood. This is no excuse, or justification for, the destructive things we do as adults. Until we (human beings) examine the effects of what happens in childhood, we cannot appreciate the excessively crazy things adults can do. "Hitler" could not have happened without the damaging events of his own childhood... Read Alice Miller.

In my case, I had to confront the reality of "religious abuse." Consider this: If "Jonny" is the source of sin and proof of inherent evil, and you hear that when you're four years old, and believe it, the consequence can create an irreconcilable split in the psyche. When Jesus is used as the contrast, against that evil within, and you believe that as a child...something weird is going to happen. No young male, in human history, has been able to prevent an erection—by asking God to make it stop. To attribute proof of evil, to an erection, is "crazy—making." I do think religious abuse is behind so much bad, or violent, pornography. In the "nature/nurture" controversy, there is no denying the effects of nurture, or the lack of it, in the behaviors of adults. To imagine that adult troubles spring from nowhere only supports the ignorant right to judge, by those who have themselves forgotten their own childhood experience. To reify "good" and "evil" perpetuates, not only the war within, but man's chronic search for an enemy "over there." Nor is this justification for blaming parents for our adult problems, but to remember that everyone has a story, so that what happens later in life cannot be seen as disconnected from the former. Freud said, "The child is father to the man." There's a koan for you.

Part of the treatment involved confronting our parents and/or significant others with the details of the abuse we experienced as children at their hands. This was a way of discharging the blame, which the spirit takes on via false shame at the mental level. It is a false shame (mentally) to attribute evil to an erection, whereupon the spirit takes on the negativity of blame and self hatred—what is wrong with me? One must face the source of negativity, and say "No" to it. Again, this is not about blame to the parents, but of asking for accountability for the healing of the human narrative.

Blame is a story, after all, and we all play different roles. Without this metaphysical background—I would eventually come to understand—the strictly psychological model all too easily does pass off blame to others. In fact, when first beginning my study of psychology, I had begun to write angry letters to my parents, seeking more details from my childhood that might help me make sense of my behaviors. Their initial reaction was to plead the blood of Jesus: "That's in the past, and forgiven—why bring it up now?" But that way of thinking had not helped me, and I had experienced the negative consequences on a daily basis. My letters disturbed them, and they considered, once again, leaving the mission field to attend to the emotional problems their second son was now stirring up in them. When Mom began to notice the positive results in my own life— the result of reviewing the past more honestly—she embarked on writing her own narratives, in support of my two younger sisters, providing them with as much honest detail about what was going on around them when they were very young girls.

My parents were unable to attend the "family week," when patients would share their childhood experiences in a safe manner. But I had prepared my "letters of accounting," which I was able to read when my parents visited, shortly after I returned to Regina from the treatment center. My wife had been able to come down for family week, and learned about her own dynamics as a "codependent."

****

We found so much hope, together, in the twelve-step program, that we felt reconciled. I moved back home with her and the kids. When my parents came, I read my letter. This proved almost impossible for my dad, who kept interrupting, every couple of sentences, trying to establish his own sense of the history. We didn't have the container of the treatment center. I grew frustrated in my attempts to read—he just couldn't listen. Mom eventually had to beg him, "Just listen, John, we can talk it out later."

Having the chance to share my perspective from the child's point of view, there was one consequence, in relation to my dad, where I felt compelled to "lay down the law" in communicating a need. In usual communication with him, he'd begin with the same question, "Son, how is your relationship with the Lord going?" The question invariably provoked my defensiveness, trying to justify some new way of thinking about life, and trying to integrate it with The Bible and Jesus. I would start to feel like a kid, searching for something to say that might please him.

As I had wandered from my evangelical moorings, however, I found that my responses could never please him. Roman Catholic and Orthodox ideas attracted me, which terrified him. "Those people worship idols, like all the unsaved do. How can you justify that?" At some point I realized I could no longer give him the answers he was looking for. So I said, firmly, "Dad, please never ask me about my relationship with The Lord again! I can no longer answer you in a way that you expect; and your question just makes me feel like a child." I said it with so much feeling and conviction, and he was able to respect my wish not to ask, "How's it going with Jesus?" The family "star" was not only as black as the older, official, "black sheep" (my brother), but he was also abandoning the faith.

I, however, was beginning to feel empowered in finding my own way of discovering a spiritual path in the twelve-step program. I was intrigued and comforted to learn that Richard Rohr called the twelve-step program "the only legitimate form of a global spirituality coming from White America." If you don't count Joseph Smith—one of my personal heroes.

9

Recovery

One blessed consequence of being separated was that I had to cook for myself. Raised in a tradition that left the cooking to servants and women, I'm ashamed to say I never questioned it. There had never been a reason for me to cook my own meals. It wasn't my place. We always had a family cook. Though we called them "servants," they were a weird extension of the family. They traveled with us to our holiday bungalows. We were to be friendly with them, but ignored them, basically. Then, through twelve years of boarding school and five years at Bible College, I lived in dorms where the food was made for me. My wife was raised in the same kind of family environment, and never once questioned all the cooking she did. It was not even a conversation. For six years, we didn't talk about it; it was her duty as a good wife. I could act out all day on the phone while my wife was at work, and when she came home, exhausted, would have to prepare dinner. She never complained.

For the first time in my life, I had to live alone and take care of myself—cook for myself! Not knowing how to start, I went straight to a bookstore, near my attic apartment, and found a new age sort of "The Broccoli Forest something." I worked on five good recipes, and honed my cooking skills: healthy meals for the whole family. So I was ready, when we were reunited, to take over the cooking and support her work by becoming the "house spouse."

****

My boss, who promised to hold my job, had to tell me otherwise. When the higher-ups got wind of my new empowerment as "a recovering sex addict," they couldn't reconcile that image with my title as a "Youth Worker." I tried to fight their decision, and grew frustrated and angry. It felt as though I was being punished for improving my life. On the other hand, I felt as though I was just "coming out" and wanted to make my contribution to the improvement of society! I didn't doubt, after coming out, that there were sex addicts everywhere. People in America spend more money on porn than they do on Hollywood and Nashville—combined.

It felt as though God was punishing me—when I was stricken with hemorrhoids, which seemed to be multiplying. Hemorrhoids are nodules of "pain in the ass!" My education in psychology made it (also, painfully) easy for me to suspect a direct connection between the hemorrhoids and my feelings of powerlessness and loss of worth—and feeling pissed off! But I could find no way to express it. I had no art, though I did take up wood carving, which I really enjoyed for a while. I really think it helped, and I have a couple of scars to prove it.

The Canadian government continued to pay for my recovery. If I wanted to keep the assistance, all I had to do was report to a psychiatrist on a weekly basis. Our sessions were like a practice in avoiding problematic conversations. With the casual demeanor of a friend, I think he really wanted me to know of his acceptance at some deep level.

****

I became ashamed of the "free money" I was getting from the government, and decided to give it up and find a job, any job. We'd both have to work. I took the first job I could: a janitor. It didn't take long for me to wonder if I'd made a mistake. The government assistance was terminated as soon as I announced that I had a job. The doctor had assured me I could have received the support indefinitely; but I cut my losses.

The janitor job involved working from 10 PM to 3 AM, cleaning a hotel kitchen and vacuuming the halls and banquet areas. It was a filthy, backbreaking, and thankless job. And the half hour hauling garbage out, in the deep Saskatchewan winter, was no joke. Regina can literally be the coldest place on the planet, regularly at forty below, and I've been out in seventy below. That's just dangerous; the air bites at the eyes, though deep in a hoody and scarf.

Given my vulnerability at the time, I could hardly have signed up for a more challenging job. Hotel kitchens are a nightmare to clean up. To keep the cooks from slipping on the greasy floors, the kitchens use huge rubber mats, at least an inch thick, with octagonal holes for catching the slop. We hosed the whole kitchen down. The smells were variously overwhelming. I vacuumed endless hallways, banquet halls, and rooms that had all kinds of pinball machines. I've still got one of those tunes stuck in my head "ta tadatada... ta!" What I felt at 2:30 AM, facing the last desolate banquet hall, really threatened my recovery. It all seemed so meaningless. Driving home at 3:45 AM, the most godforsaken time of night, I felt tempted to pick up the hooker who so often patrolled the street I drove down to get home.

Working as a janitor did give me an insight. If God had a job, it would have to be that of a janitor. First of all, when other employees don't show up for work, the place can still function; but if the janitor doesn't do their job, no way, the place is unworkable. The kitchens would be unusable. There would be nowhere to put the garbage coming in. Customers would walk back out as soon as they saw the mess. Janitors, furthermore, must be invisible. Every act the janitor makes is calculated for staying out of the way, and getting the job done as efficiently and quickly as possible. A good janitor can work without anyone noticing. No one notices a good janitor; like the gorilla (that no one sees) on the basketball court. And janitors suffer the slings and arrows from late night drunkards. When the bar empties out, one of them will not resist pulling the plug to the vacuum—from down the hall and around the corner to the outlet.

When I come across a janitor today, like those in the nursing homes where I work as a CNA, I make sure to tell them, "If God had a job s/he'd be a janitor." They understand. Someone has to clean up our mess, unnoticed. Anyway, after a year I got over my God trip about being a janitor. I had to find something in line with my education and real interests. The spiritual discipline required of a janitor was too much for me; I needed some less meaningful work.

****

So I got a job with the Salvation Army at a home for troubled kids. It surprised me to find out that they were using corporal punishment, and I was to accept it as part of the job description! At that time, I was still sympathetic to the concept of "spanking" your children, so I didn't have a strong objection. The two Salvation Army women who ran the place, took that part of their job seriously; and I could hear the beatings. I felt a strong objection building up inside me, like there was something "not right" about the use of spanking. And I hoped I'd never have to do it. The kids soon realized that I was a pushover, and paralyzed in my ambivalence toward corporal punishment. They took advantage of that, knowing that I might not spank them the way the two SA women had. But one night I got angry and spanked one of the kids, as prescribed. The kid was unbroken, and mocked me. That terrified me, for I knew I'd become an abuser. The sense of guilt was so strong that I decided never to do that again. When I told my wife about the experience, we decided right away that we would never spank our kids. We even told our kids that we would never spank them. But I didn't think that I should argue with the Salvation Army, so I requested a meeting with someone at Social Services and told them that the Salvation Army was beating their kids—and I had done it.

Thereafter, I got a job as a "counselor" at a lockup unit for teens. And the same thing happened, just on a more "professional" level. They said I was expected to participate in "take downs," which could happen more than once in a day. Takedowns were required when a kid gave even the appearance of aggressive behavior. They would tackle the kids and then strap them down on a special bed, or throw them in the "pink room," a room with soft rubber walls where the teens could throw themselves around, and scream as loud as they could.

One day, I begged for a chance to try another method. So I walked over toward the remonstrating teen and sat down, leaning against a wall. He kept shouting into the air, right next to me, as I just sat there and listened. Eventually, we were able to have a conversation and he calmed down. As far as I was concerned, it worked.

However, they thought that my approach took too much time. "We don't have all day for you to sit around talking with kids." Other staff were troubled by the inconsistency in methods. They warned me that I'd lose my job if I didn't participate in the take downs. So I went along with the expectation, for a while. What I learned about myself actually surprised me. I have access to a store of adrenaline that is fearless and eager for a fight. The energy itself was an adrenaline release that excited and empowered me. I even felt eager for more! I did not know I could feel so calm in the face of fear and aggression—confident that I could take them down. But my conscience bothered me. I began to notice how the other (especially) male staff had developed a pattern of egging kids on, to the point where a "take down" was inevitable. This seemed more like a bad habit than a legitimate treatment for teenage problems; and I was ready to quit yet another job.

****

I heard about a Catholic retreat Center in Saskatoon called Queen House Retreat & Renewal Center. After a couple of retreats there, I got to know the director and shared my interest in dreams with him, and that I had facilitated dream workshops. Queen's House offered a wonderful variety of retreats. After Vatican II, the Roman Catholic Church had changed dramatically. It became my impression that Catholics, from before that time, had experienced the RC Church very differently. Some terribly conservative elements seemed to have softened substantially. I'd heard horror stories from people who'd been educated by nuns. It always sounded, to me, like the same malicious woman. Someone with a long stick/ruler, eager to smack you on the head or knuckles. But what I found was a Church that was remarkably open to all kinds of expressions of faith. One of the retreats I attended was led by a monk from a Carmelite monastery in Crestone, Colorado. He was a convert from a Protestant tradition, and in a private conversation, he informed me, "The Catholic Church has the Reformation." Queens House offered retreats in Feminine spirituality, Liberation theology, dreams and Jung. They offered a retreat on handwriting analysis! They were even open to the pentecostal movement! Mother Church, embracing her lost children. So my experience of using dreams in therapy, and facilitating dream workshops, fit right in. He put me on the schedule to lead a retreat based on dreams.

Most of the retreats I attended at Queens House centered on contemplative prayer—and lots of silence. I was attracted to the concept of "contemplative prayer." So before attending my first such retreat, I thought I'd get a taste for it by driving to an area just north of Regina, called the Qu'Appelle Valley. When you drive north of Regina, along the featureless highway, you'd never suspect anything but more flat and interminable landscape. Yet when you reach the Qu'Appelle Valley, it's like entering another world. Suddenly the earth opens up and you drive sharply down a hill into a beautiful valley with trees and a stream at the bottom. I thought I'd go out there, drive off the highway at one of the pull-offs, and walk into the "wilderness," "the desert." I wanted a taste of "contemplative prayer," and silence, or something of the experience of "the desert fathers."

Expecting peaceful reflections in such a bucolic environment, among the low bushes, gentle aspens, deer and rabbits, the sound of birds twittering sweetly, the bugs buzzing in the warmth of the sun—surely I would feel the closeness of God and achieve some deeper spiritual revelation. Well, after just two hours, at the most, I was oppressed by lust in the worst way. It felt as though a chain had been placed around my neck and would drag me back into town to make phone calls, breaking my "sexual sobriety." I could not resist and felt really stunned and helpless at the awful incongruity around my expectations. The irony made no sense. I marveled at how the silence had evoked the very experience I thought it would relieve.

The same thing happened a month later when I went on my first weeklong silent retreat at Queens House. By the third day, I couldn't stand the silence for another minute, and rushed downtown, where I got a room, drank some beer and made some phone calls. When I came back the next afternoon, I fully expected the director to let me know that I was not a candidate for the contemplative life, and that I would have to leave. When I told him what I'd done, he laughed and assured me: This is exactly what to expect in a first confrontation with deliberate silence.

He reminded me of the Desert Fathers and why they went out to the desert in the first place: to confront their own demons face-to-face. He suggested that it's only in silence that we really see our unfinished business. It was my willingness to face the silence that allowed me to see so clearly the depth of my resistance to the inner world. It was more a call to notice—than to change anything. He was so accepting and nonjudgmental, encouraging me to take in the experience as an opportunity to notice and maybe even find some humor. His attitude and acceptance felt healing. I had been so serious about my problems—real life and death issues to resolve. He encouraged a simple willingness to embrace my fears, and lust; and that I did not need to understand everything on the spot. Encouraged, I went out the front gate for a walk, and suddenly felt my heart break as I kicked a little stone down the sidewalk in front of me. Through my tears, I began to sense a loving relationship between me and that little roundish stone! I couldn't explain—something that seemed so dumb. But once again, love was present, like that gaze between my daughter and me, now between me and a dumb pebble!

****

One of the books I read during this time was Bradshaw's "Healing the Shame That Binds You." I had a twelve-step friend who asked if I'd like to accompany him down to Billings, Montana, to hear Bradshaw speak. Bradshaw was being sponsored by The Rimrock Foundation in Billings, a treatment center for all kinds of addiction problems. After one of the meetings I was chatting with someone who turned out to be the Director. I asked her if they had a treatment program for sex addicts. She said they were currently working on it. When I told her about my education, my own experience at The Golden Valley Health Center with Pat Carnes, and that I had initiated a twelve-step program in Regina, she immediately suggested that I consider coming to Rimrock to work! I could hardly believe my ears; and of course I was thrilled to say yes.

When I returned to Regina and told my wife about the job offer, she was also happy for me. Anything that helped me feel empowered would be better than slugging along, working at jobs that were not satisfying, which seemed to threaten my recovery. I was even able to renew my US passport, which I thought I'd lost for good when I became a Canadian. Then the Rimrock Foundation even offered to help with all our moving expenses. They also suggested a realtor who could help us in finding a home. Finally, I would have a job doing the very thing I had been trained for, and dreamed of—since having failed as a missionary. Now I'd be a real psychotherapist, getting paid to work compassionately with people with addiction problems: alcohol and drug addicts, codependents, people with a gambling addiction...and sex addicts.

The first thing they wanted me to do was become very familiar with their model, which meant working my way up from the admissions departments, then doing evaluations, assisting primary clinicians, and finally being assigned a therapy group of my own.

In addition to attending a small and growing Sex Addicts Anonymous group, I had also quit drinking and was attending AA meetings. Eventually, I found a group where mostly old-timers met to discuss topics. The focus was not so much on newcomer stories, which I didn't feel so comfortable telling, not having much of a "down and out" AA story to tell. I had been drunk a few times, threw up half a dozen times, and had a few hangovers. But I just didn't have the kind of crazy story of battling alcohol, compared to what I knew about lust. Neither had I any experience whatsoever with any other drug, and didn't smoke pot until I moved to Boulder, Colorado—which is ahead of me in this story.

The AA crowd seemed uncomfortable with me sharing details of my sex addiction. They tolerated it, but didn't want to talk about it themselves. I learned that, for a lot of people in AA, "thirteen-stepping" is pretty common. Why not pick up sex partners at AA? They didn't want to have to deal with that conversation, so I hardly talked about sex at AA meetings. However, the topical group was a great education, and informative for my work as a counselor with alcoholics, etc. It's amazing how much wisdom you can glean from people who've been talking about "resentment" for thirty years! I love the "No Crosstalk" rule at twelve-step meetings. You can really express yourself, and let it go, knowing someone isn't going to come back at you for what you'd just said, good or bad—just listen. A story does not need to be fixed, just told and appreciated for what it is. The "After Meetings" also gave me a chance to develop connections and deepen conversation.

At any rate, I needed one good story to tell about my relationship with alcohol. It happened during the end of my time as a Youth Worker. The whole team of Youth Workers was on a work-related retreat at a nice hotel on a lake in northern Saskatchewan (where there are actually trees and lakes, not just endless prairie). I'd been drinking more and more at the bars, and could easily handle four to six beers in an evening, a couple times a week, without feeling hung over the next day. On the retreat, my boss had requested that he be billeted with someone calm and quiet, as he needed to be rested for his leadership role... so he asked me. I didn't have a reputation as a hard drinker and seemed, to him, like a pretty level-headed guy. I did not know what a rowdy drunk I could be. We were given the last day and night of the retreat off, to relax and party.

I started drinking in the early afternoon and kept it up till early morning. The tab later revealed that I'd had sixteen beers. When the bar closed, a bunch of us were hanging out on the lawns behind the hotel, and one of the guys had a bottle of rum, which I demanded he share with me. I had not learned about the drinking "principle:" do not drink harder liquor after drinking beer or wine, though you can go the other way, from, say, rum to beer, but not from beer to rum. I do remember him mentioning, "watch out for that—it'll be fire." It was just another drink to me.

He and I proceeded to walk up and down the halls of the hotel, provoking the other social workers—asleep in their rooms—with songs and comments about their characters. When I finally stumbled into my room, I made it halfway across the floor and sank into a squatting position. In that comfortable pose, my mind provided me with a convenient image: that I must have been sitting on the toilet. Assured that I was in the right place, I let go, bearing down for a good one. The sense of relief was satisfying, for a brief moment, until I tried to get up from "the toilet" and found it cumbersome. Then the smell came to me, then a squishy feeling in my pants, then the horror dawned on me: I was nowhere near a toilet, and had just shit a doozer in my pants.

My boss suddenly turned into an angel of mercy, and rescued me from hell. He effectively carried me into the bathroom, and helped me get changed and cleaned up and into bed. He just kept encouraging me, in my shame, regaling me with stories from his own troubled past, assuring me that he had "been there." I don't know how he cleaned up that much shit. I was devastated and humbled by his acceptance. But I have never had such a hard time getting my body out of bed as I did the next morning.

We were supposed to be out of the room by noon. I had thrown up a number of times, charging from my bed to the balcony. The bathroom was too far, and I'd puke on the carpet. When I finally made it to the back seat of someone's car the next day, in a daze of alcohol poisoning, I vowed that I'd never drink again, and go to AA meetings. It was an experience I didn't want to repeat. I wouldn't drink again for the next five years, and when I did I found that I never needed more than a couple of drinks—to bolster my desire to dance. But hangovers were no longer worth it.

****

I was learning a lot at Rimrock Foundation. My sex addiction recovery was not perfect, but I was feeling pretty stable, with the occasional slip into pornography and masturbation.

I renovated a room in our basement where I could see my own clients and facilitate dream groups. Working with "the inner child" became more and more of my therapeutic focus. In the treatment program, the focus had been on helping clients clarify written assignments about their addiction use history, which they were expected to read in the group. There was little focus on connecting the emotional wounds, of childhood and society, to the various forms of "acting out." I had the conviction that oppressed emotions can fester, and find new ways of "acting out."

My troubles with Rimrock started when the administration began to hear clients screaming from our group sessions. I'd encourage some clients to pull on a towel as I held it firmly at the other end—to express a repressed desire for closeness with someone they felt abandoned by as a child. Or I'd bring a mattress into the room, and pillows, and have them read their letters to abusers until they felt a rage come up in them, enough to grab a pillow and start beating the mattress with it, screaming out their anger over what had happened. This was not acceptable form, in the Rimrock model, and they started putting another counselor in the room with me, making sure I stuck with the script, not veering into the underlying emotional energy/issues.

****

I'd stayed in touch over the years with another MK from India who had also become a psychotherapist. He mentioned a book by Ron Kurtz' called "Body Centered Psychotherapy : The Hakomi Method." Eager to explore all forms of psychotherapy, especially one recommended by a trusted source, I bought the book. It was another turning point in my life. Here was another moment, like reading that With magazine article on masturbation, Thomas Merton's "New Seeds of Contemplation," and Pat Carnes' book on "Sex Addiction." I soon heard about a therapist living in Boulder, Colorado, who had partnered with Ron Kurtz in developing The Hakomi Method. After absorbing the book, it felt clear to me that Hakomi would become my approach to psychotherapy. I called the Hakomi Center in Boulder and signed up for an introductory weekend workshop for prospective students.

Driving into Boulder was itself an experience of "coming home." Boulder had an aura that felt laid back and accepting, like anything could happen. There was something inherently creative in the air, a sensation I hadn't experienced, yet knew must exist—somewhere in America! I fell in love with Boulder. It was like a pocket of interesting life—surrounded by "American sprawl."

To be accepted into the training, prospective students would attend at least one four-day session. The goal was to discover a commitment/or not for the training, and for the trainers to evaluate our potential to do the training. I was eager.

The organizer had asked another participant, Matt, if he'd be willing to put me up in his tiny apartment at 7th and Pearl. No problem. He lived a couple blocks from Dot's Diner, and the famous Trident Book and Coffee. Matt and I would take an instant liking for each other, and we became fast friends. He's the kind of man I can hang out with for hours, never tiring of conversation.

It took me a while to get used to the laid back atmosphere of the Hakomi crowd. People sat around on "backjack" chairs, lounging casually with each other, touching easily, leaning on each other for extended periods. I'd never seen anything like it. In my memory, the only people who showed affection in public were married or obviously dating. And even then, not casually.

I not only completed the two-year training—once a month, Thursday night to Sunday night—but also functioned as an assistant for a further two years. There followed another full year in a program called Group Leadership Training, which applied everything I'd learned in Hakomi to the Group Process.

Driving back to Billings, after that first Hakomi Training, I found my right hand touching my chest in a gentle massage, sensing a dialogue developing between my body and my mind, like they were seeking forgiveness of each other for some sort of ignorance and misunderstanding, or some kind of ancient mistake. I realized how little I had listened to my body, or respected its needs and capacity to communicate directly. I had treated it so much like an object of fear and lust, the source of all my problems; when the real problem stemmed from mistakes in my own thinking toward my body. I wanted to learn how to listen.

****

Half way through the two-year training program, again driving back from Boulder to Billings, I stopped in Casper, Wyoming (the suicide capital of America) for the night and found myself making phone calls from my hotel room. I connected with a young woman who came right over, and without further conversation, we had unprotected sex. She seemed OK with that, smiling happily as she left. But I thought, "Oh, I'm in trouble now," and once again would have to confess to my wife, especially since I'd had unprotected sex. I didn't want to risk passing on some STD to her. I imagined that the young woman was promiscuous herself. When I told my wife, she insisted I get tested for STD's and refused to have sex with me for three months.

In those days, it took weeks for test results to come back; and I would use the time to meditate on the possibility of having AIDS...and death. I had witnessed, twice, the decline and death of people in SA who had contracted AIDS. But I had never before seriously contemplated my own death, aside from those suicidal moments of madness. Now I had this whole gap of time to face that fear directly, and leisurely. There came a moment, standing in front of the kitchen sink, washing the dishes after dinner, when I was struck by a very weird kind of "fear." It was a kind of nothingness; and I wasn't thinking of Sartre, or feeling philosophical; and it wasn't pleasant, and didn't feel meaningful. It was not a fear of hell or punishment or hope of heaven. There was simply a wall of nothingness. I would be nothing; just not be; not be here. No one could touch me and I would touch no one. It didn't matter what might happen after death—I would not exist. It disturbed me. It felt repulsive; certainly not reassuring. It seemed to me that no belief system known to man could help me face the facticity of simply no longer being in the world; and that any concept I might have had, of a "life after death," offered no consolation.

Whether I was dying or not, something had died in my wife. She'd taken the time to think about her own life, and was projecting into her sense of a future with me. She wondered how long she would be OK, forgiving me and tolerating my behavior. What if this was still going on in fifty years—could she accept that? It was clear to her that she'd reached her own limit. I knew her well enough to sense when she'd made up her mind about something: there was no changing her conviction. She asked if we could go on a hike along the trail near the cliffs that separated the lower area of Billings from the area above. She wanted to have a conversation. Her mind was made up. It had been fourteen years of dealing with my sexual drama, even recovery drama, and she wanted to take the kids with her and move to Victoria, BC, Canada, where her parents lived.

At some point, towards the end of our conversation, I stopped along the trail to pee. She walked ahead. Absorbed in my thoughts and feelings, perhaps even a vague sense of relief, I was almost done peeing when I looked down to notice that

91

I'd been peeing directly on a curled-up rattlesnake, basking in the sun on the rocky ledge beside the cliff. It was so blended in with the rocks—I hadn't even seen it. Amazed, I wondered why it hadn't moved—at all—but lay there as though enjoying my golden shower. Talk about dream symbolism!—but of what?

10

A New Direction

The most satisfying thing about being a parent was our bed-time routine with the kids. It could easily take two hours. First, we read from a stack of library books. We went to the library almost every week. I loved reading to my kids, tucked around me or on my lap. As they got older, and just before the divorce, we read through the Lord of The Rings trilogy. After reading, we lit candles and went through the liturgy for the evening, learning the call and response. While marriage felt psychological, the bond with the children was a tugboat in the liquid of my cells, their bodies like appendages growing out of my stomach and heart. This sensation was not on-and-off but a 24/7 alertness to need.

A year into our family practice with the Catholic Liturgy, Mom and Dad came for a visit. During our devotional time, Dad prayed in the Evangelical, conversational tone: talking with The Lord about things. In the middle of his praying, Cara, a second grader, leaned over to my wife and whispered, loud enough for all of us to hear: "Why is grandpa giving a lecture?" I felt something between an urge to "crack up," and feint. She had, with bold innocence, put words in my mouth. How often had I heard the prayer, "Dear Lord Jesus, help Teddy to be a good boy."

My son acquired a huge Lego collection, a new batch with every birthday and Christmas. I had as much fun playing

Legos as he did. We typically played games in the evening (we had no TV), we read library books, then we had family devotions before brushing their teeth and the bed time routine. We took time with each kid. As I put my kids to bed, I sang tunes I'd made up for the twenty or so Psalms that I'd memorized. We'd then chat for a while as I gave them a light back rub as they dozed off to sleep. Nathan would lie perfectly still, but Cara was bouncy. She played to the end and laughed till it was hard for her to breathe. So, the nightly routine had become the most important thing in my life. I couldn't wrap my mind around the death of our daily routine, like the corners of my world were crumbling. Those were the hardest days of my life.

We discussed our divorce plans for a month. The kids didn't know, and in every moment I felt a cave of aguish, how precious they were, how innocent: I watched them play, peal an orange, brush their teeth; I watched them sleeping. The inevitability of it didn't bring any relief. My mind started looking for a metaphor for the pain. I thought of my face at the center of the pain, and a fan that would slap me, at first, fast and repeatedly. O, this is happening... O, this is happening?... This is happening... As the weeks went by and the day finally arrived, the pain and sense of failure struck me less often, but it was still relentless.

The time had come, finally, to tell the kids. We would do it in the evening around dinner time. When Cara came home from school that day, she did what she usually did: got a snack and chatted about her day. I watched her little hands peeling the orange like it would be the last memory of my life with her, and I'd never see her peel an orange again. Little pieces of orange peel, her little hands, her bubbly conversation, full of trust and innocence. I thought I'd break to pieces. Later we had the fateful meeting and told them I would no longer be living at home, but nearby, and they could come over to my place on the weekends. We said the words quite quickly, to get them out and over with, like a death sentence being read. There was no consolation in that family meeting, just suffering and anguish. We all cried. I remember the tears and the confusion and the quiet resignation. I was grateful for the routine that carried us through the evening, "It's time to brush your teeth..." I felt guilty, and a sorrow I couldn't hope to understand.

Research led us to the conclusion that it was better for the kids to have one home, not two. My wife would represent "home," and I...would leave...on a prodigal journey...for the heart of White America.

Sometimes I think nature has a program that conspires to bring children into the world. Love was expressed by the fact that we woke up together, every day, and brought two beautiful children into the world. We were a success. But psychologically, we were both facing the historical fact that we would be the first couple in our ancestries to have experienced divorce. It was hard to admit how therapeutic the movie "Mrs. Doubtfire" was for us at that time. Hollywood to the rescue? How can experience be reframed when you have no tradition for the experience? I guess that's what "going into uncharted territory" means.

Perhaps Cara experienced the deepest kind of pain. It's one thing for a parent facing the moment of separation—having had a little preparation and some awareness of what's going on. It's another thing for a seven-year-old who trusts her father to the ends of the earth. As a young married woman, we finally talked about what that experience was like for her. I felt another kind of heartbreak when she shared how my absence felt like an "endless gap." She'd held on to the idea that I was away for a while and would return at any time. Like Dads who go off to war: they come back—some day. Her therapist suggested, as one consequence, that she doesn't look for a father figure, and more easily accepts men in her life as they are.

I'm not sure, really, how my son dealt with it. He's a quiet and "deep water" character, and, like my daughter, we still connect and he doesn't seem to be consciously troubled by what happened. Yet, when I think of how close our bond was, it stings to think about it. We always loved our conversations about the "meaning of life." He was so curious, always probing through the surface of things. He asked wonderful questions. When he came into the world, that was the first thing I saw about him: his face all scrunched up in a big question mark, forehead wrinkled, his eyes peering up and all around in a sort of freaked-out-wonderment... like "What the...?" We played soccer together; I encouraged his imagination. So it felt to me as though we lost something we could never retrieve. I had waved goodbye as he went off on his own voyage into the unknown, but without a father for a guide. I'm the prodigal... father.

****

We remained in Billings during the first year after our separation and divorce. I rented a room from an elderly woman in a mobile home park. She was my referral from the RC Church. Smoking cigarettes, she regaled me with wild tales from working days as a dancer in a bar. She drove a pink Cadillac.

The Catholic Church I was attending, and engaged in the Rite of Catholic Initiation for Adults, offered me a little room where I could see clients in my psychotherapy practice. On one occasion I was referred to the Crow reservation to offer a workshop on dreams. The Crow men invited me to my first sweat. I thought I would die, but they actually encouraged me to beat myself with a soft grass "switch." That made it really sting—at first. The effect was ironic, both increasing the pain, and yet, by persisting to whip myself—partly angered by their persistence that I "use the switch, use the switch!"—I became empowered in facing the pain, and thus able to endure it. I'll never forget that. And standing naked in the snow later, oblivious to the cold—that was sublime. When do you get a chance to stand out in the snow, impervious to the cold?

****

We were grateful to the Roman Catholic Church when she blessed us with an Annulment. Our Protestant marriage had been performed in ignorance, and God wouldn't hold that against us. What a mercy! How thoughtful of Mother Church! I remained an ardent Catholic for three promising years, and fully expected my romance with the Roman Catholic Church to continue... when I moved to Boulder. Attending a different RC church every Sunday, for four weeks, I was earnestly hoping for one of them to draw me in, but I felt as invisible as ever. An intruder, wandering around aimlessly, waiting for someone.

The fifth Sunday came and I'd run out of Roman Catholic Churches in the Boulder area. I was up and dressed and ready for Church, like every other Sunday of my life. It was another beautiful day in Boulder, and I was sitting with a coffee on a chair in the little living room, the sun shining in, it was brilliant and crisp. I saw the Flat Irons in the distance. I felt suddenly stunned, when, from out of the blue, a neighbor began blaring—at full volume—"Onward Christian Soldiers, marching as to war, with the cross of Jesus going on before...." It was the very last thing I expected to hear in Boulder! But a surprisingly weird thing happened. It struck me—with the swiftness of a slicing sword—as a death knell to my whole Christian trip. I could never attend, seriously, any Christian Church—of any kind—again. But wait... is ACIM a Church? Is Unitarian Universalism a Church? I would attend a few of those meetings in the years to come.

****

It didn't take me long to start looking for a girlfriend. I met a Rubenesque young woman who wanted a lot of sex. I'd begun to wonder if only men are actually obsessed with sex, that perhaps women were really not interested after all.

While fully expecting to charge back into shameless sex addiction, as I had in our first separation—in fact, my sexual panic began to subside. It had seemed, almost immediately after getting married, that if I wanted sex, I had to initiate it. I would try to be disciplined, and patient, and longed to be as sexually content as my wife was, imagining that if only I could be happy without sex I'd be a happy man. It never happened.

My urge to make phone calls diminished remarkably. And because caller ID had brought the portcullis down on my ability to make anonymous calls, I would have to make do with what "normal" people did with lust: porn, masturbation, and girlfriends.

****

When I moved to Boulder, I took the first job I could find that might be satisfying: working with kids at a place called Kindercare. Maybe I thought being with kids all day would fill an emotional gap left by not having my own children around. But working with a room full of four-year-olds is a study of human nature, the quintessential, and differentiated, expressions of the pure human beingness. Children younger than four are mostly small masses of physical dependency and need. Kids who make it to first grade are quickly transformed into social and psychological aficionados, conditioned within a year by all the basic rules of human social behavior.

But four-year-olds are still bursting with uniqueness and innocent curiosity. They come tumbling through the air, on play—or not—mode. They've found their feet, like Olympic athletes, and can use their hands to their full potential. Each one of them moves through space with a notable difference; they follow no outer authority but the flow of interest within their bodies. Flowering, for these few moments of time, they each reveal a true, unique expression of the human animal, untainted by the intense conditioning fields around them. You have never seen a four-year-old walk through the mall like an adult. Real human beings do not walk or move the same; no one walks like George Bush unless they've been forced to walk that way. Real uniqueness shows itself shamelessly. We break our children: "Walk normally!" "Don't spin, you'll get dizzy and fall down." But a four-year-old doesn't think about fitting in. They're bundles of self-expression, and self interest. If you want to visit the most interesting zoo in the world, observe a group of four-year-olds in one room, or on a playground. When those same children turn five, they disappear; they climb into the wallpaper, the stuff that hems us in and corals us all into "normalcy."

****

Mom and Dad had returned to India for one last visit. They'd retired and were living in Vancouver, BC, and flowering in their Evangelical faith. They attended a charismatic church close to the University campus. We still felt some sort of spiritual connection. Our family had attended a charismatic Alliance Church in Regina, so I was familiar with the Pentecostal experience. During my brief stint at the Alliance Bible College in Regina, we had hooked up with an acquaintance from the Bible College in Toronto who had also attended U Waterloo, where he studied for a Phd in Church History.

He attended this charismatic church, where he was an elder—and invited us. We did attend, and stayed long enough for me to become an elder. Until a woman I had connected with on the phone, and to whom I had divulged, informed the pastor of the call. The pastor called me in for a meeting with the other elders. Feeling defensive and cornered, I tried to assure them that I was getting therapy for the problem. The experience helped me understand how hard it is for people in leadership positions to come clean about problems, especially sexual problems. Maintaining the image requires emotional rigidity. Scandals tend to shatter things. Think of Jimmy Swaggart... think of so many gurus and teachers and politicians...think of someone you know. Think of Lance Armstrong. Moral failure, from a position of privilege, is not easy to admit, and I was not ready to tell my whole story to the pastor and elders. I was asked to step back from my duties as an elder, and could no longer offer communion.

So my parents were finally on a similar track with the charismatic experience, raising hands in song and singing praises for an hour, reaching a kind of emotional climax with the speaking in tongues. I was hoping for the gift of tongues, and had learned—made up—a few incomprehensible phrases, using them to chime in as we wept in devotion and repentance before the Lord. Mom and Dad had become involved in the church's "Training for Ministry," and people loved them. They spoke honestly about their experience as missionaries, and perhaps a few of the students even heard the story of "the accident."... "We were broken before The Lord."

****

Mom had returned from India with a "bowel condition" that wouldn't go away. She went "from doctor to doctor, but nothing helped." When finally diagnosed with ovarian cancer, she had only weeks to live. Someone called to tell me that if I wanted to see my Mom, while she was still alive, I should come "asap."

The week I spent with Mom (and the whole family) was my first experience of attending to someone as they lay dying. For two or three days, she was able to speak clearly, if slowly. We had always enjoyed sharing interests and insights, and had agreed, long before, that she would share everything she could, as long as she was able to communicate. She began to drift in and out of "states" I deemed to be visionary. One of these astonished me, a kind of blessing and benediction on her relationship with Dad. She opened her eyes wide and, looking over at Dad, said, "O John, wasn't that wonderful!"

He had no idea, and asked, "What happened?"

She reacted, "You know, you were right there with me! We were brought together before the throne of The Lord. I said to the Lord, see this man; I have forgiven him, but it seems he has—still—not heard it directly from you! Could you please tell him, now, that he is forgiven?—wasn't that wonderful, John!" John could only weep. It was a revelation just for him.

****

Mom lapsed into hours of deep, relentless groaning. Then I did something that I have since learned should not be done: hold a dying person by the heels. In my ignorance, I was keeping her grounded, making it hard for her to let go, turning her groans into determined and persistent grunts. Meanwhile, a number of church members came over and began praying and singing, as though to cover over her groans. They went on and on until I finally asked them to stop and just listen to her groaning: "The most profound praying we will ever hear!" And in our silence we did listen, and we heard the ancient prayer of the Psalmist: "O lord hear my prayer, o lord hear my cry, when I call, come to me." That's what I heard. I really let it sink in. Dad found the ongoing groaning hard to bear, and needed a break. So I suggested we go out for a walk. We were away for only ten or fifteen minutes. During our walk, I shared with Dad something I'd recently heard about love: that in this world, the mundane world, love is also a burden. Love binds us to one another in a way that can feel choice-less, and heavy. And when that burden of love is released, there may come, along with the grief, a feeling of relief. They said it was important not to confuse the relief—release from the burden of love—and blame yourself for feeling it.

101

When Dad and I returned from our walk, we learned that Mom had "passed away." My sisters were there. After we left, she had grown calm. Her groans must have been saying, "Teddy, let me go!" They said she became very quiet and peaceful, looked over to the family pictures on the wall, then closed her eyes a final time. We took it as a call to sing, to wake the neighborhood with evangelical song! How we wanted to sing for Mom! We sang a bunch of our favorites, in spontaneous harmony at the top of our lungs. Great is thy faithfulness... O love that will not let me go, I rest my weary soul in thee, I give thee back the life I owe that from the ocean depths its flow may richer, fuller be...

After that, I felt a deep need to go off by myself and be alone. Maybe, I thought, in the depths of such a profound moment, perhaps God would make Himself close to me, and provide some conversation. Or was I just talking to myself, after all? I remembered Mom as a mystic. And she was by far the better speaker. In fact, she was so insightful and funny, and really brilliant when she spoke. When it became apparent to her (and others) that she eclipsed my Dad as a speaker, she went silent and completely stopped speaking at meetings. Later in life, she would speak again, a fierce, penetrating spirit full of grace. It was Dad's missionary background that formed my bible story. I don't know where Mom came from, and she herself was raised as a missionaries' kid from somewhere in South America! I'm ashamed of the fact that I have so few words for her story. I've been wounded, and glorified, by the patriarchy—at his end.

While pondering my mother's life, I walked until I came to a park bench, and once again sat there in the sun—unusual for Vancouver. One of the things my Mom had shared in the week before she died, was to review, for each of us, her sense of where she saw, each of us, going forward. As usual, she started with David, then Margi, then Joy, and finally me. Then she made a gesture, mirroring a pattern we were all familiar with when in the progression of one of her rare fits of rage. This would happen when she'd finally had enough of all of us, and she was ready to give us all "a piece of her mind." We knew, in the momentum of her rage, that we better just be quiet and listen; even Dad would sit and listen. Her passion was exquisite, accompanied by sharp finger pointing. In one of her outbursts, when we were children, Dad had slapped her—the only time I remember anything like that. It was such a shock to us all. I had never seen him do that before, nor would I again.

I don't remember what she had said. I see his hand suddenly dart out, the sharp sound of the slap, and her bursting into tears. Ordinarily, every other time, when she went into her rage, we all knew it was best to sit and listen. So in the momentum, she would finally get to my turn, and launched in with... "And you, Teddy!" ... nothing. A pause for reflection, stirring up something, then she would cry. She could never articulate precisely the scolding I was dreading to hear. Once, just once, when she didn't think I was around, she was making an audio tape for David, recounting for him our day to day life in India. He was still in high school in Minneapolis. I overheard her saying... "and Ted can be such a pain in the neck!" She really annunciated... "such a pain in the neck!" I was astounded! What... me? I didn't respond, but I was going over in my mind what I could have done to make her say that. I really didn't know. At any rate, before she died, she was sharing hopeful words for my siblings. Then she looked slowly to me and grew quiet, once again, her eyes and face in a gesture of peering into the future... to no avail. She just shook her head and sighed. "I don't see where Ted is going... but he is in the hands of God."

Hearing the words "in the hands of God" brought forward another series of memories. I remembered my grade twelve annual school book. The members of the graduating class were each given a full page to fill, however they liked. My roommate and I placed ourselves sitting crosslegged in a pair of hands ("the hands of God"). I have my right hand up in the evangelical "one way" sign, while my head is turned left to a picture of Ruth, hidden in the branches of a tree! The irony didn't escape me, even at the time, sensing the division of my desires. And then, I also remembered what I'd said in grade two, in response to the teacher's question, "What do you want to do when you grow up?"—and not having a clue but "Whatever God wants me to do."

It seemed appropriate, in that moment, sitting there in the sun just after Mom's passing, that I should pray. I wanted to pray. I wanted to commune with God. I needed someone to share my deepest feelings with. Prayer was always an honest way for me to pour out my feelings. Now, sitting on the bench, I felt nothing toward/from God but a determined silence. The awakening I'd had in Taos left me without a conversation with God. My ship had lost its moorings—to the language of the Christian Church—and sitting there, the loss felt very real. I could not bring myself to believe that I could honestly have a conversation with God—as "someone out there." And just when I most needed that consolation. I felt alone—in a new way—and sensed once again my abysmal loss of words.

The End of Religions

I won't forget the mystical woman I met on the plane while traveling to be with my mother for the last week of her life. We made plans to meet in Salt Lake after Mom died, on my way back to Boulder. Romance really is like falling into a novel—whether thick or thin—with the intensity of teenage emotions of "Biblical proportion."

I don't remember who started the conversation. We looked into each other eyes, smiling with intrigue at each other. Her eyes were those "limpid pools of mud" (a phrase I love), and her hair was long and wavy and brown. We fell for each other in a flurry of spiritual words. We talked all the way from Denver to Salt Lake, where she lived. She mentioned in passing that she was in the process of separating from her husband.

Kate was a connoisseur of new age spirituality, I was never sure exactly what she practiced, but she felt destined for something "higher," but didn't know; maybe I might have something to do with it. We were both vulnerable, and open to a new experience in relationship. I wasn't sure if I'd ever see her again, but she assured me she'd meet me at the SLC airport whenever I returned from Vancouver. And there she was, walking toward me in a light blue knee-length dress. I think it sparkled. After fourteen years of struggling to ignore all occasions where I might have enjoyed the experience of falling in love, it felt wonderful to let myself tumble into that delicious first blush of romance. The special someone—I surrender; can I look into your eyes and drink you up?

I think female, and gay sex addicts, can find "easy sex" almost any time they want it. But straight guys like me tend to be the "perverts," having to do more outrageous things to satisfy the urgency of lust. At any rate, I was ready for a new kind of risky behavior. So, a month later, I drove from Boulder to SLC for a rendezvous with Kate. I imagined, all those hours driving, that she would spend that night with me in my hotel room. But she couldn't spend the night, and in fact only had "six minutes!" How desperately we kissed. She couldn't clear her schedule with her husband and two kids. She couldn't just disappear for the night! She assured me she still wanted to be with me. The next day, I drove the 517 miles back to Boulder. What was I thinking? I drove a thousand miles and more for a a few minutes of desperate kissing.

As it turned out, Kate was offered a job in Denver, and her parents lived in Lakewood. She left her husband with her two young teenage kids, and moved to Lakewood. The relationship lasted an ingestion period. She came to realize that she'd left her family prematurely, and had to return to them. Now I had a taste of someone leaving me, when I wished they'd stay.

****

Sometimes, emotional issues build up to a perfect storm. The week that Kate left, Dad announced his engagement to Elizabeth, one of my teachers from Sunrise School in India, the one who'd spanked me a few times. She was the teacher who would show us pictures of Kali, and then contrast that image with the blessed Lord Jesus on a cross.

Actually, this part of Dad's story is amazing. He's a lucky man. The story came out that Elizabeth had fallen completely in love with my Dad, from the very first time she met him. She must have been the same woman I heard laughing the night he dropped me off at Sunrise School. But Elizabeth kept the secret of her love for my Dad. She said she "never spoke to a single soul of it," until she finally "confessed" her love for Dad in a conversation they had after Mom died. She had remained one of the many missionary friends my parents had stayed in touch with. It was only in conversations, after Mom died, that she divulged the secret she had kept to herself for forty years! Other missionaries had often asked her why she remained single. She was attractive. Her answer was always the same: because she was in love with a married man, and, therefore, he could not be emotionally available to another woman. And it was not right for her to interfere in a relationship the Lord had ordained. She was a virgin when she married Dad! Now, come on, I think that's a great movie!

Dad had finally won his princess, and experienced a happy marriage. And I was really happy for him. There was no reason in the world why I should object. But when they came to visit me in Boulder, on a kind of honeymoon tour around the Western US, the encounter was not at all satisfying, a little scary. I had the feeling Elizabeth wanted to drive a demon out of me. She could not have approved of my spiritual condition, and Dad must have said a few things to warn her. But I was still in the emotional trance of meeting my parents—together—with Mom as mediator. Dad tried, always, to keep spiritual talk simple and centered on Jesus. My probings never came to a point or a conclusion. So I could always challenge Dad's position—as long as Mom sat there, curious and open to new ways of imagining the Scriptures. I think Mom had a secret interest in secular literature. Not so with Elizabeth. I began to sense her bristle as "we" launched into our "family" conversation, sharing our latest insights in our "walk with the Lord." But before we got too far, Dad turned to Evelyn and said, "It's better not to argue with Ted—you can't win." He knew my penchant for provoking and challenging conversations about faith and religion.

The moment reminded me of what I'd lost with Mom's passing: her mystical openness and curiosity. For Elizabeth, everything was black and white and settled by reference to The Bible. A Puritan. The portcullis came down on our conversation. And so I also lost my sense of connection with Dad. But what could we talk about? I have always felt incapable of "normal" conversation. I'd never had a conversation about "the weather." I drove away from that Indian restaurant feeling as though I'd also lost my Dad. I realized how much I had depended on Mom, in order to connect with Dad. I know I still have some things to process in my relationship with Dad. Perhaps "Dad" is as big an issue for me as "the patriarchy" is. I like to imagine "The Patriarchy" as the theme of our Human narrative—and, excitingly, in the last chapter. So my story with Dad remains unfinished... because I'm still living it out.

****

My familiar bonds to the past were quickly breaking down. When Mom died, my Christian world was crumbling. I was freshly divorced—accepting but painfully missing my wife and kids—and my new lover left, all within a nine-month period. Fortunately, I was involved in the Hakomi Psychotherapy Training with Phil Del Prince in Boulder. All these issues came to a head just as we were learning how to create ceremonies for "grief work."

The training itself provided a healing structure for my emotional process. The ritual I designed for my own grief process had two parts. First, I wanted all the men to hold me down while I would struggle against them, and try to get up. I really wanted to unleash my anger and grief within a safe container. I wasn't convinced the men could contain my feelings—and that no one get hurt. I was partly motivated to extend the application of "contact improv" as a dance form that might be helpful in meeting human, especially male, anger and aggression. I had been trying to hold in and manage an energy that trembled inside me. In a circle of fellow therapists, sitting on "backjack" chairs, my outstretched knee caps would always tremble and bob. It was embarrassing. I'd have to cross my legs and bunch up to control it. I didn't know if I was nervous or scared or excited or what.

If I attended to it, as a good therapist should, the shaking would threaten to take over my whole body. The nervousness energy felt strong and as alive as an untamed animal. It had an edge that felt out of control, and I wanted to let myself feel the full strength of that energy, while not hurting anyone, or getting hurt! So the guys held me down while I struggled. It felt delicious to struggle with all my strength, and feel held at the same time. I let the sadness and the fear and anger come to the surface—let the demons rage, I would be OK. In the second part, I asked the women to lift me up over their heads and march me all around the room while I let go into their arms, taking in the comfort. Finally they lay me down. Let me tell you—a lot of pent up men could benefit from such a process today.

****

Finding a new spiritual path was exciting. I was learning to meditate a la Trungpa Rinpoche: "the path of the Shambhala warrior," the possibility of "crazy wisdom," the simplicity of "just sitting." Buddhism made so much sense to me. I loved Trungpa's writings. And I enjoyed the wildness of his followers. So, I began climbing the endless ladder called Tibetan Buddhism. After a year of Meditation Instruction, I began the Shambala Program. We met once a month for three days of teaching and sitting practice. It felt grounding. I didn't experience anything I would call "enlightenment," but really felt a delicious attraction for the discipline of "just sitting meditation," especially during the longer periods. I began to sense a calm clarity, the sweetness of attention to what's there, learning to embrace what happens as it does.

****

While still living in Regina, my wife and I had attended a number of seminars on The Enneagram. The Enneagram is a profoundly useful tool for understanding the dynamics of the human ego. I forget the name of the couple who taught it, but they knew Ichazo and Naranjo from the training they received in South America. The Enneagram struck me as a powerful tool for self knowledge.

Ideally, you learn which Character you are by learning the whole system at once. As I reflected on each Character, separately, it was the "specialness" of the Four that eventually got to me. I felt "pegged," like I'd been found out. "Fours" feel special. No kidding! Astrology told me I was a Virgo. But that didn't mean anything to me at the time. Astrology seemed too general, and the details intimidated me. There are so many kinds of Virgos, and I never identified, at the time, with the idea that Virgo's can be perfectionists, or with being neat and tidy. Me? Neat and tidy? Not on my desk. OK, I do use a large wet wash cloth for a daily bath. Showers are overrated. And I strongly prefer women who are clean, and who wash their dishes. Anyway, I'm a #4 and always will be. To be human is to play a Character. In accepting my limitations, I was beginning to experience what "freedom" meant—to play your Character properly!

When you study The Enneagram, you go back to the ideas and practices of Gurdjieff. People wonder who Gurdjieff was and where he came from. He brought The Enneagram from out of some Persian desert—and taught it to The West. "Meetings with Remarkable Men" reveals the mystery of Dance according to The Enneagram. But when The Western world published The Enneagram—The Body Disappeared! "What Enneagram are you?" The dance of The Enneagram ended when the Mind Game took it over. The Enneagram has been colonized by the Mind and has lost its Feet.

I wanted more than just the psychological understanding of The Enneagram. I wanted to work with it in my life. So, when I moved to Boulder, I went searching for a Gurdjieff group where I could do "The Work." I went to half a dozen different Gurdjieff groups, each with a different style and emphasis. I was, once again, shopping for my perfect "Church." Every Gurdjieff representative I met with tried to convince me how they represented the Gurdjieff lineage. How was I to find the original practitioners?

Finally, I made contact with a carpenter who represented "The Gurdjieff Foundation." They didn't invite me to a meeting, as a first step, which I'd prefer, but to meet for a one-on-one with a man named Larry. I met Larry at his carpenter's work shed. He was covered in dust and a suspicious wisp of alcohol. Midst the clutter of tools and wood and dust, we sat and talked. He never changed the subject from "What's your question?" I wasn't sure what he meant, and I don't remember my response. He said, "Until you find a real question, why engage in The Work?"

All I could say was that I didn't know what my real question was, but wanted to do The Work to find out. I think my first real question was: "Why don't I know what my own question is?" I was impressed with Larry's style and earthiness, and he invited me to a newcomers meeting.

****

At my first meeting, I wasn't sure who the newcomers were. Two or three people were standing close to the wall, perfectly still. Five or six people were sitting quietly on metal chairs. There was no talking. An uncanny bunch, serious. For three entire years I remained the only consistent "newcomer."

I returned each week to sit on a metal chair for ninety minutes and listen to readings from Ouspensky, and Gurdjieff's "Beelzebub's Tails."

The chairs felt harsh, and demanded a determined posture in order to endure the hour. It felt like a kind of torture, some Kenyan endurance test for kids. After a year of reading Ouspensky, they started reading Gurdjieff's "Beelzebubs Tales." I was forbidden to make comments, and was only to ask questions. And above all, no laughing. Do you know how hard it is not to laugh at some of Gurdjieff's stories?! Like the guy who lived at a train station in India, whose job it was to wake the whole town up every morning with his loud bell ringing. In order for him to deal with the wave of resentment he felt, coming back at him from the townspeople—as he woke them up—he first prepared himself with a ceremonious series of curses. It was hard not to laugh—I could really imagine that guy, and the curses.

During my second year in the Gurdjieff Group, they invited me to a full-day "work session." A famous higher- up Gurdjieffian would come and teach. I began to learn the dances. It was nerve-wracking; I was in first grade again. Standing in six or seven lines (I should remember), we were to weave our way across the room in a mathematical sequence, while moving (in my case, waving) our arms in specified ways. The instructions were assumed, and I'd have to learn by just doing it. I think the point was to remind me of what a fool I am, and to keep starting again. The other dancers would shove me out of their way, and I'd slop my way over to an assumed position, pure guess work. I was at the blackboard in mission school again, but now I was motivated to endure the shame of my limitations.

I was, finally, invited in for the Full Work Weekend, which culminated in a banquet. I arrived a few seconds late to my first such event, and the doors were closed. I was not about to be left outside, and started banging (with determination) on the door until someone let me in. She didn't say anything. I guess they figured I should be rewarded for wanting in so badly, as to make such a shameless fuss. I wasn't about to walk away politely.

They assigned me to a committee called "Setup And Takedown" (SUATD), the committee I would remain on for three years, and never did graduate. I remember a weekend when I worked with a group who were assigned the task of making wooden meditation kneelers. Meanwhile, regardless of the particular small group we were in, we all had the same overarching instructions: for example, focus on the difference between your left hand and your right hand. Or, "Every time you hear the word ‹I' come out of your mouth, how do you notice it in your body?" We were all aware that everyone, no matter which committee they served on, was focused on the same attention practice.

I learned a lot about the value of Setup And Takedown, where the intention is to serve, clearing the wary, creating the setting, and cleaning up afterwards. We were to make sure the setting was a place for The Work to proceed smoothly: pick those things up and move them somewhere else; keep positioning the chairs for changing group configurations; be on hand for any need whatsoever that may arise from the whole environment; set the table for the banquet; when there are undirected moments, keep in mind: "they also serve who only stand and wait;" then, "bring those," "arrange that," "carry these over there," "go get those things and set them up in the room over there," "bring the equipment in from that vehicle;" when it's all over, put everything away; fold and stack the chairs; roll up the carpets; clean up. Gurdjieff always emphasized the importance of the setting for communicating spiritual ideas. When and where, and how people hear, is at least as important as what the message is.

These "work weekends" culminated in a banquet, every item of which was the result of our conscious work together.

The arrangement, the food, the entertainment, the drink; everything was planned and created during the work periods. I felt overwhelmed with gratitude during the banquet, every time. There may be a kind of group spiritual orgasm in such practices. So many deeply mundane moments, culminating in a beautiful banquet, including a choir presentation. I felt the touch of each of the various contributions. I had never experienced such a moment in my normal White American world.

I invited my girlfriend, Jackie, the Buddhist Meditation instructor, to a party sponsored by the Gurdjieff Group. We were to invite family and friends and potential inquirers. It was not intended to be a "work" situation, but a time when we could relax, have a beer, eat some food, and talk about stuff. But not "Work!" So Jackie and I got some food and were hanging out.

As I looked around, I noticed how all the Gurdjieffians were definitely engaged in some kind of "work mode." They all looked serious. It started to feel weird. Did I miss an assignment? Jackie even noticed it and made a side comment. I thought to myself, "Can't they pretend *not* to be working?" Did they need (yet another) practice—"how to appear ordinary?" Come to think of it, the ability to appear as ordinary should be a skill mastered by any who would claim "spiritual practitioner." But I'm a #4 on the Enneagram, with a #5 Persona and #3 Shadow—so I tend to (want to) tear the masks off. I saw the masks, ubiquitously placed, on the "serious Gurdjieffian." Why such seriousness, exuding from all of them? Was the "Work" hardening in place, like a mask? That's when I found my question. Do I have to be serious? Do I want to be stuck, interminably, in a "Work" mode/posture? Has "The Work" become another (bad) habit? That killed it for me, right there.

Now, I have huge respect for The Gurdjieff Work! It seems to me, when I hear other "new age" types talk about their particular spiritual path, I'm not sure what they *do*. Gurdjieff

Work can offer Westerners a taste of the practical environment required in which to develop a spiritual practice. Most of us White People are all alone. Knowing this, Gurdjieff resurrected The Enneagram, (a synthetic—Revealed—formula in itself) around which he oriented his followers. He applied The Enneagram as a tool: for thinking through things, for movement/dance exercises, and for structuring group-related events. Then through all ordinary living situations, train the mind to pay attention in specified ways. Though we may all have been involved in different activities, we were simultaneously engaged in the same mind training.

****

One of the women in the Gurdjieff group liked me. She'd been raised by first-generation Gurdjieffians and played a leadership role in the group. She took me aside, before our next Work session, and right away stated that I should appreciate the once-in-a-lifetime opportunity she was about to offer me. I'd been invited to a Work Period with Jacob Needleman on the West Coast. He and his wife had facilitated one of the Work weekends, and I had been reading his books. He doesn't advertise his connection to The Gurdjieff Foundation. Yet even as my friend asked, I knew my answer was No. The experience at the "Party" had shown me an image (like a final product) of The Work Group. I did not want to see myself that way. Poised in space, dully attentive. I'd been raised by serious missionaries, and I was ready to throw up "Serious"—like a false god I could no longer stomach. If I'm "serious," let it be for the sake of *play*! I had been developing a theory, that "seriousness" is the tell-tale symptom of human spiritual sickness: all the issues of blame, and who deserves it. The actor, that I am, appears to be serious at times. I cannot tolerate negativity. But I sure can bring it into the open. So I have the impossible task of explaining that it's not serious, because I'm acting my part in The Play.

****

Jackie (who went with me to the Gurdjieff party) was my first experience with a lover who was also a friend. Before we came to know each other, I had put her in the "unattainable" category. Popular and respected in the Buddhist community, she taught a meditation class at Naropa. She loved to laugh. I can still hear her outbursts in my head. She was an attractive part of my engagement with the Tibetan Buddhist practice, the Shambalah Program. Sitting every morning, memorizing the Heart Sutra, I could sense the calming and grounding effect of "just sitting."

I was also building my psychotherapy practice as a Licensed Professional Counselor. I didn't know if I was some kind of western shaman, or just a Pharisee helping people make peace with Rome. We used codes like the DSM to frame our thinking about troubled people, the criminals, the disabled, the mentally and emotionally broken. As a Licensed Psychotherapist I worked under the direction of The Justice Center, and I translated the law of Caesar to the masses in servitude.

****

My work for the Justice Center gave me a chance to clandestinely teach Buddhist Meditation to the guys in the drunk driving program. I substituted the standard "twenty minute Relaxation Technique" for "Buddhist Meditation." summarizing what I'd learned at Karma Dzong after fifty talks on meditation. What is the best way to "just sit" comfortably for twenty minutes? How and why get interested in doing just that? "Get as comfortable as you can, as straight as you can, and try not to move." Buddhism gets religious about posture.

When you meditate, you gotta sit right. Or you're lounging and thinking about things, reading at best. In meditation, you first bring your mind to the attention of feet-knees-hips, elbows-hands-shoulders, with your back as straight as possible. Look down between the knees (since they were sitting on chairs, not zafus). Give your full attention to your in-breath, and on your out-breath—let go. Focus foremost on the breath. But that's not the point, the muscle is developed by merely noticing when you are Not paying attention to the breath, but wallowing in the idea-opinion-mystification factory. The muscle is further developed by bringing the wandering mind back to the breath, and then finally to rest in the Splenic awareness within the breathing motion practice.

While The Buddha taught equal attention to the in-breath and the out-breath, Trungpa said, "Know you are breathing in on the In-breath, but on the Out-breath, just let go a puff of air in front of you. When you notice your mind thinking about something besides breathing, first label your thoughts with 'thinking' and bring your attention back to physical breath sensation—and so to your body. The short-cut here is to merely notice your thought as the way of return. Don't judge your thoughts at all, but try not to run off with them. The Buddha was tricky: Don't cooperate with the demands of The Maya—just sit—and watch the madness happen. Isn't that comedy? When you are watching a movie, don't interfere with it at all. The Buddha gives you the only correct human perspective, in terms of how to just look through your own eyes in the now of the body. The Buddha is seeing your own life right now from a compassionate meditation room on top of your crown. Your soft spot, where Now looks through you.

My boss must have heard that I was teaching the guys at the jail some alternative to the required "Relaxation Techniques." So he came out unexpectedly and sat in on my class. I merely tried to clarify the simple instructions and why they are important in meditation. What became clear to all of us—as we just sat there for twenty minutes—was that he was the only fidgety guy in the room. He couldn't help but be impressed. "How did you get those men to sit perfectly still for that long?"

I responded, "Twenty minutes is an eternity when you have no experience with forms of mind training. I told him, meditation is a human right.

****

As I began to find connections around the Psychotherapy community in Boulder, the Mental Health Center asked if I wanted to assist in the development of their Sex Offender Treatment Program. I was directed to a committee at the Jefferson County Courthouse, responsible for creating a State approved model for dealing with sex offenders. They were all in agreement that there was no such thing as treatment for sex offenders; sex offenders were mere criminals. What I discovered was a room of women (fifteen women) and one other male. Fifteen angry women and one punishingly angry guy—to champion them. I dared not challenge them with my "Addiction Treatment" model.

I started to wonder, what it would be like for a battered woman to show up at a shelter, only to find a group of men at the door. I had heard sex offenders talk about what it's like to go into a group for the first time, only to face an angry female therapist. And they were wondering why the recidivism was so high. When the woman I worked with at the Mental Health Center found out that I called myself a "sex addict," I lost my job in a flash. I requested a meeting with all the staff, refusing to just walk out the door. A number of the staff were ex-alcoholics, working with alcoholics. I remember wondering how they might find the experience of being an alcoholic helpful in the treatment of alcoholics; but when it comes to sex, the therapists were to hide their own sex life in a sacred closet, never to be spoken of. Human experience is really hell (unrelenting torment) when there's no one to tell your story to, and when the world teaches you to keep your unbelievable story to yourself. That's not healthy or right.

****

Unable to thrive in my private practice, I took another job with The State. I wanted something easy. So I got a job as a "live-in" at "Chester House." Three autistic guys, living with three... "normal" guys. Michael, a friend from the Gurdjieff Work, was already working at Chester House, and he recommended me for a job as one of the roommates. Michael was a breath of fresh air. The first time I saw him, he strolled into one of my early Gurdjieff meetings holding a giant pillow, which he placed on the hard metal chair—and sat on it! I was waiting for him to be admonished, but no one said anything. Then I thought he was purposely challenging the group norms. Or maybe he was told to bring a big pillow and see what the new guy does. He was a painter, another Four on the Enneagram. His latest piece involved filling his canvas with the tiniest strokes of paint possible.

And then Don arrived—the third "normal" roommate—a new Naropa University student from Iowa. Like a new enthusiastic covert, he was eager to take up a serious meditation practice. He talked a lot about wanting to "get more into my body." Michael and Don were not the social work/therapy types. The three autistic guys lived upstairs, while the three of us were in the basement. No matter what the guys upstairs were doing, Don and Michael were impervious. They didn't clue into suspicious sounds or behavior. They hadn't had children. I was feeling like a parent again: training for staying awake on the job. You're on the hook all the time. You have to listen, wait actively, be prepared, then offer calm and a sense of safety and nurture.

With the autistic guys, I would wake to the slightest vocalizations or creak in the floorboards. Chip was no trouble, though I heard he used to be a terror. Something had happened to shut him down. He was a little black guy. He moved with quick and jerky movements, and then he'd stop and hiss

119

and look back at you as though from under his armpits. Rich was a water nut. Always washing his hands and drinking the water from the tap or from the hose outside. Then he'd snap his fingers and act agitated. It was hard to intervene with him. He could whack you, or act like he might, or smile sweetly and just keep going. He was the only one who really made me nervous. Even though David could bite you, as long as you stayed out of reach, he was too slow to get to you. And David made his daily contribution to the house with a loud and punishing masturbation routine.

Pretty soon, I was beginning to learn the acoustic elements, like a song. "Peewpeeepee... pip pip... umff... whup whuuup pew pew umh umh.... He was an artistic savant. He'd draw tiny figures on paper, color them in and cut them out. I mean, really tiny. Tiny fingers on the thinnest limbs; all kinds of different cartoon-like characters. I was convinced that if anyone could market his art, he'd be a millionaire. Art, with such diligence, is a thing that should be recognized and rewarded. I later heard that, in fact, someone was helping him in that direction. We saved all his art in big garbage bags, a ton of it. He didn't seem to care what became of it; he just kept drawing his figures and cutting them out carefully.

David was also a vicious headbanger. He could smash through the wall plaster with his head, and he knew that, so he'd lumber outside and get down on the ground on his knees and bash his head down on the lawn, bloodying it. What a perfect image for The Nightmare: a man smashing his head into the earth. We did our best to slow him down, but then he could bite you.

****

Don soon met a man who went by the name Ra Uru Hu. I thought, "Yah right, even for Boulder that's over the top." I didn't yet appreciate the true arrogance. People who live in

Boulder eventually take on Hindu or Buddhist names. I didn't trust the gurus from India, or the Tibetan Lamas. I knew people in Boulder who went to India for a few months and came back wearing holy robes and giving talks on enlightenment. When Don asked me to meet Ra, I said no thanks. I've got Gurdjieff and The Enneagram, The I Ching, Trungpa, Jung, Dances of Universal Peace, Dance Home, Psychotherapy practice, trading massages—my hands are full.

When Don came back from the planetarium (where Ra gave his talk), it seemed as though he'd had an electrical shock; something had obviously blown his mind—and he had to tell me. What I heard sounded pretentious, and I was really spooked by the thought of a "Grandmother Voice" communicating with Ra through a vertical beam. Apparently, Ra had experienced the Voice for eight days (and nights)—straight. He was told about the origins of our universe, which, he claimed, is not a "Universe" but a Female Entity—still within the Womb of The Mother! This was some cosmic fairy tale! He said The Human Design System was a formula for reading human nature, and nature per se.

But I was settled in my spiritual path, Trungpa and Gurdjieff, The Enneagram and Dream Analysis, and a smattering of other esoteric ideas. Every Friday night I went to The Dances of Universal Peace, but I had the most fun at Dance Home. We met in an old vacant warehouse (at the time) on the west end of Pearl St. All we needed were a few huge carpets placed over the hard cement floor. We put on the music and threw our bodies at each other: men, women, all together, it didn't matter. With eyes closed, there's only The Body and its delight, after all. We wanted to explore movement and gestures, the theater of dance—in the most creative ways human beings could imagine. My friend Martin flung himself through the air. I learned to fall on purpose, over and over. I began letting my body do the talking.

We were doing what would become known as Contact

Improv. Start by exploring movement with someone by only touching hands to elbows. See how much you can do with just that. So I was feeling satisfied with my spiritual life, and my sexual life, and Dr Bob Unger was supervising my psychotherapy practice. I was really feeling satisfied, at the top of my game, and the future seemed to be opening up for me. After all, I was in Boulder, Colorado, enjoying the cream of the White American Dream.

****

But Don couldn't stop talking about this Human Design System. He wanted to see my "chart," but we didn't have the technology for calculating it. So he used an astrological ephemeris and plotted the information on my Body Graf. I think it took him at least six hours to plot the twenty-six positions on the Body Graf. Today, you can plug in your DOB, time and place, and get your own chart for free in a second. Don looked at my chart and kept saying, "Wow, look at all that energy."

I was struggling with the change in my relationship with Don. This young, intelligent, but somehow inept kid was now the one giving the "spiritual" teaching. Yet everything he said about the HDS Information was... hard to argue with; and how uncannily personal the descriptions were to me. A few of the descriptions felt more like a problem to be overcome, not blatantly embraced, as Ra dictates. I'm "rigid," "cut my losses," "weak ego,"... it gets worse, "shaking hands with the devil." These were not the words I wanted to hear about me, because I keep in mind the worst information first. Like a heart that says, just for now, we have to allow Israel to be A Camp, or the world of humanity will never come to The Gathering. We need a party scene, Israel, not a boring old war zone. We can deal with the alcoholics, ignore the alcohol.

However, out of the blue, Don decided to ditch his life and went searching for Ra in Ibiza. He bought a one-way ticket to

Europe, hitch-hiked to Findhorn, where he stayed a day, and then on to Ibiza, where he found Ra. Ra said he could take his tent and camp nearby in the woods, and help him make audio cassette recordings for some of the first talks he would give on The Human Design System.

****

Not long after, Jackie and I had gracefully parted ways, I met a sex-crazed yoga instructor. I must have needed an even deeper healing. There were times when I really wanted to sleep and had to wrestle her off threateningly. Lust is rapacious—as a human energy it's not personal. She wanted a threesome with her not so ex-boyfriend. Once we got down to it, I was surprised by my lack of enthusiasm. Or the difference between my ideas and... I don't know, but Jonny was not interested. They urged me on to fuck with gusto. I was embarrassed. In my awkwardness, I imagined the gods enjoying themselves at my expense. This made me laugh, which didn't help. They asked me to leave. Maybe good sex, for me, involves the passion of negotiating a bond into conscious awareness, serving whatever purpose can be found in that bond.

****

After Don left, I found work as a family therapist with Alternative Homes for Youth. Don't quit your job until you find another one, ordinarily. I abandoned my other roommate and the three autistic men. I consoled myself, knowing I was easily replaceable. I felt like I was on top of the American dream, in my sweet little apartment near the top of The Hill at 7th and College. My own place, my own practice, the most beautiful view, a bird house on the tree. The large front window looked out on the mysterious Flat Irons. Honestly, I never tired of looking at the Flat Irons. The jagged shadows could tell the time of day. The sunset sets twice on Boulder, and off the surface of the Flat Irons. When it snows a little and clears in the afternoon, it's like a fresh Bob Ross painting. The same scene magically changed.

I built a New Age Tibetan Buddhist Shrine before my front window, where I could see the Flat Irons through the tree. My shrine was an evolving collection of the nine archetypes for The Enneagram. I found a quality plush Persian carpet, and had all my sessions on the floor, sitting on backjack chairs. Regular clients were coming, I facilitated a little dream group, and was deepening my therapy practice in the Hakomi Method. I was being supervised, in a group of other therapists, by a master who used the Modern Analytic Method in his supervision. I did The Matrix Training for a year. The co-founder of Hakomi, Phil Del Prince, had asked if I would be an assistant in future Hakomi trainings. I was jazzed.

Lust had become a manageable nag, centered on complicating my already sexual relationship. For example, I had encouraged Jackie, before we formally broke up, to have sex with a guy who liked her, an old friend. How would I know what an open relationship was like, if I never had one? There was a lot of talk in Boulder about open relationships. Lots of experiments, and small cult-like communities. My favorite cult was a Gurdjieff-based practice applied to running competitively in a 100-mile race. They won. Meanwhile, in a strict routine, they were to swap partners and begin again without delay. You're tempted to say holy fuck.

Anyway, Jackie was up for it. But I wanted more control over the experience, as though I should be involved in how it was going! But she was out of my hands, and it freaked me out. I tried to make her call me, just to tell me he was there, and they were just about too... She didn't respond to my calls. Jealousy, or lust, or whatever, had an effect on my human physiology akin to mental torture. Relaxing was out of the question. Jealousy is the best cure for sleep. It should be bottled as a tonic for staying awake. Simultaneously, it was like being locked in a jail cell for something you don't understand—and you want out bad. But you can't do anything. The emotional wave grew into criminal resentment; with a readiness to crash through the social barrier. At five in the morning, I marched over to her house and walked straight into her bedroom. He said to call the cops. We talked it through. I learned that lust and jealousy are two sides of the same coin. My memory is essentially the history of a sociopath. For good or bad, Hu knows.

****

Don finally did return from Ibiza. He was away for at least a year, and when he came back, he was different. Not the kid I knew, but calm, and mentally sharp in a way that unnerved me. I still wasn't interested in examining my own chart. I wanted to know what he'd learned from Ra about consciousness and awareness. But Don was tethered to Ra's dogma, "No Choice." He added, "You're not responsible." He was so calmly persistent in his position I got defensive. What do you mean, No Choice? Of course I'm responsible!

I was so determined to understand what Don was talking about that I rented a room for him and gave him money for food. I was obsessed, with finding out what had happened to him in Ibiza, and why The HDS had become so important to him. It was my intention to test him and prove him wrong. No Choice? It felt like I was fighting for my spiritual life. Slowly, he refined his message to "You don't possess a choice." And, "You are not responsible for your responsibility." It turns out "responsibility" has its own nature. Big deal, what does waking up have to do with No Choice? I asked, Isn't there a practice that comes with HDS? He just said, "Look, love yourself." His coldness bothered me; he didn't react to my heated resistance; he giggled at my struggle. But he showed me a lot of respect, and he understood that I had to struggle—with a life and death energy—when coming to terms with meaning in my life. Don was challenging the very foundations of meaning in my life.

One day, Don came into my apartment and announced that Ra would be in Taos in a couple of days for a ten-day session. He was planning to start teaching the Human Design System in the United States. It was my turn to make the leap of the fool. I called Alternative Homes for Youth, where I worked as a Family Therapist, and told them I wouldn't be coming to work for at least ten days and would accept the consequences. I was surprised when they agreed to give me the time off. I had to meet this frightening man, Ra Uru Hu, who'd done something to my friend. Yes, it would be the end of the story of Ted, like "Choke Your Dreamer," and the beginning of...

12

To The Fool

Ra Uru Hu offered his series of teachings on The Human Design System in a Taos Hotel. Don and I stayed at the home of a Taos shaman whose house was a good three-mile walk north east of Taos. You can have the best conversations, and arguments, on long walks with a friend.

Ra talked without notes. He used a projector to show the aspects of The System: the overlapping I Ching and Astrological Wheels with a Nine Centered Body Graf in the Center. The Membrane and The Cell. He would introduce us to The Ajna and The Entity. Ra had lived in a "ruins" on the Island of Ibiza. He said his "*ruina*" had been built over an ancient well. It was in this *ruina* that he experienced a terrifying transmission from a "grandmother voice." The Human Design System was part of the revelation. The Voice called him "Ra Uru Hu." He was a French Canadian, and I think his name had been Robert. Anyway, for eight straight days and nights, Ra had received a download of occult/mechanical "facts" about... what I had called "the universe." I think he knew the information was meant to be shared.

Part of me felt nervous, not only being in the presence of a mad man, but also the stunning, new perspective on... everything. I couldn't have imagined that I'd listen to someone who claimed authority from "a voice." Yet Ra sounded clear and endlessly interesting. He couldn't bore me. As he lectured, explicating the "visual science," I was seduced by the coherence of the formula. I'm fine-tuned toward religious claims, eager to question them. He wasn't trying to be a guru or a spiritual guide. He had simply received astonishing information, and actually felt obligated to share it, as a "human right."

He embraced No Choice—and preached it. He recognized how the HDS was a language that revealed the uniqueness of every human being, and that the goal was simple: "Love Yourself." Each of us has integrity, and knowing it can protect us against the human disease of "self hatred," and the forces of conditioning that cause us to become "normal." Here was an explanation of real Human Rights! I became tickled by the idea that we play a real character on the world stage, that we've literally been given our lines (in the I Ching), which we can recognize in ourselves, and come to love who we really are. Then it doesn't matter what happens—you are OK with who you are in this dream. This was the essence of what Ra was saying to me.

It went on like that for two or three days—until I started feeling nauseous. In fact, the vomiting started on the third night of the training. We'd walked back to the shaman's house, and after dinner, Don and I continued to discuss Ra's presentation. I found myself gazing into the kitchen table-top, which had, fortunately, been cleared. The air was turning into water. The Universe was disappearing, and in its place—a female entity in the womb of The Mother! What am I? I had been concerned with old questions: What happens at death? How can I work on myself? What should I do when I grow up? All the unanswered anxiety came on with a wave of nausea. And then I saw wheels within wheels—the solar cell that we exist in. The nausea grew.

The shaman got nervous and gestured to Don that he'd like to leave. Don looked a little too cheerful. It was about time Ted got cracked open. Payback of sorts. As I sat there, transfixed on a geometry I could see off the surface of the table, Don went to get a bucket and a mop, assuming it might be needed. He stood with his mop to the right of the big, freshly cleared table top. He kicked at the bucket and said, "Well, you get to have a body!" My attention narrowed on the surface of the table. It turned into a 3D arrangement of planes, my attention directed to a point in the center. It felt as though I was hurtling through space, from the direction of Virgo, no less, toward the center of the wheels and the planes. The sense of speed and momentum slowed as I approached... (the center?). Then the image changed to become an endless series of incarnations of Homo sapiens, layers of them and increasingly under pressure toward the approaching center of the geometry.

On another scale, I felt a push from ancestors, and something like a voice encouraging me (finally!) to break through.... Ted, break through! Get to the other side! But something in me rebelled: I would not play that game! A "NO!" (not a no of fear, but a "choice"): Not to seek life after death—not to seek an afterlife—say Yes to This Life! As the No burst out, so did the vomit, bouncing off the table of geometry. And the vomit felt like the burden of the past, all those religious expectations—rushing like a herd of demons through my body. I can see the vomit arcing through the air and splashing over the mirror. Don cleaned it up while I sat there stupefied.

It happened again the next night. I was in the middle of a large empty room, leaning back in a recliner, contemplating the teachings of the day. Again the nausea came. This time I could imagine the whole Solar Cell as a kind of clock, a cellular clock. It made me dizzy. And then I heard a phrase Ra had said in passing, "Jupiter, Lord of the Raves." The phrase seemed to light an electrical storm in the heavens. It came like a thunder bolt and was heading straight for me. Struggling out of the recliner, holding down the vomit, I made a bee line for the door, which, fortunately, opened with a push. Imagine another fabulous arc of puck traversing the frame of the door.

Happily, it fell harmlessly on the rocky driveway.

The next afternoon, I had a full-blown—out of the blue—satori experience. I was feeling physically weak and trembling. I could tell my body needed comfort. And I wasn't looking forward to more frightful vomiting. The shaman recommended an almost secret hot spring on the Colorado River. We would have to hike down a treacherous little path. It was perfect. We took off our clothes and got into the deliciously hot water, mixed with occasional coolness from the river. The sky was blue and crystal clear, and we were alone. Don sat across from me, looking east while I faced the west. We talked about the nature of consciousness, etc. I still wanted to settle this issue—before I could embrace HDS. Perhaps I needed another conversion experience, thick skull that I am.

As Don continued with various explanations, he suddenly lighted on a familiar metaphor. When I saw the picture he suggested, casually, my old life as "Ted" came to an end. He said, gesturing, "It's as though your life is in a soap opera, and you are one of the characters." Then he raised his hands in the gesture of a video frame. "And then one day you hear something and your perspective shifts"—while he pressed his hands away from his face. "You're still in the same movie, but now you're looking at it from a different place."

I can't tell you the exact sequence of events; it seemed to all happen, at once. Whether I had been moved two inches (what it felt like), or a foot, or a micro gap, my perspective was viscerally shifted. I went from being ensconced in the scene, to watching the scene from a physically different place/perspective. In other words, precisely as Trungpa had said: "Watch the movie!" But now I really was watching myself as an actor on a stage! Two other things happened at the same time. I heard Trungpa's high-pitched laugh, and a huge gong sounded across the heavens! The final piece, which may've been the first, I saw a Golden Buddha suspended in the sky above Don's head. The gold was deep, seemed solid, and had depth and outline. I started to giggle. I felt the laughter as a bubbly spring of water that wouldn't shut off—for days—it's still there. I'd wake up at night and the giggling would return. The relief I felt then was enormous, and it spanned the whole sense of my life from beginning to end. I was OK. I am OK. I will be OK. There truly is nothing to do and nowhere to go.

****

The Fool in me was awakened, and the fool needed a new name. Everyone in Boulder has a spiritual name. Sometimes old names don't work. "Theodore Leavitt Garrison:" Gift of God, messenger for the priesthood, strong place for his people... was not enough? The sense of "Ted" would become a fond memory. An almost normal person, sincere, earnest to be good. Failing, feeling bad, trying harder. A careful listener. A patient psychotherapist. A wallflower, shaking in the stem. A guy who always felt split and hypocritical: calm and cool on the outside but seething with something and uncomfortable with metaphysical uncertainty. "Waheybi," however, threw all the trappings off with a flourish.

Waheybi the Fool. Waheybi was like a never-ending explosion of madness. He was also celebrating his fantasy of the 60s, a "freedom" he had been denied. He was ripping off his covers. Waheybi followed his inherent curiosity. He was determined to experience the world, as fresh as a wide eyed child, intent on play, challenging obstacles. But in the thrill of throwing the past off, Waheybi had no time for the central teaching of The HDS: Follow Your Strategy and Authority! To wait for a sacral response before acting, and then patiently allow the emotions, time, to process. Waheybi knew only that he was OK—and so everyone must be OK! What he had experienced was surely something to be shared, and way too exciting to be contained!

I returned to Boulder two weeks later to discover that I

had indeed lost my job as a family therapist. And I wouldn't work again for at least ten years. I was in no position to follow orders, or have a regular routine. I was busy climbing into my new vehicle, my body. The Universe had literally disappeared and I was now inside an enormous, living Entity. In fact, an Unborn Female Entity. This became my Gospel message: the Unborn Entity! It astounded me that this Vision was not seen by humanity, and I felt compelled to communicate it. It was hard for Waheybi to feel compassion for the generally sick version of life most people seem to live in. Waheybi wanted to vomit all the religious paradigms and scream: "Be The Friend!" and "See The Baby!" All the boring religious shit—just see The Baby! We'll stop killing each other when We do! I wished I could snap my fingers (like a magic trick) and make The Universe disappear—and people would just see The Baby-Ranie! There She is!

I fully expected the happy news I brought back to Boulder would open all the doors for me. So I put all my clients into one group. I was done with the games, I wanted them to leap. I wanted them to see how, even their problems have integrity, and can be read in the Body Graf. Now, Don and I would use their problems and point out, ironically, how much integrity they have! Look, your solar plexus is open—of course you're fucked up! You never realized that all your emotional wave comes from other people!

In the few years before meeting Ra, I had gravitated in my group practice to the Modern Analytic Method. So I wanted to really work with that form in the group. Don is a natural witness. With corresponding charts on the floor in front of him, he sat in a corner of the room. At the end of the session, he reflected on the emotional conflicts in the group in the light of the various Body Grafs. We were looking for integrity, made evident in the problems. I was excited. Group Psychotherapy—with two witnesses. But my clients were upset because I would no longer meet with them individually. I couldn't do it. And they didn't care for the "chart thing." They had lost the comfort of a good listener. So I fired them all.

I tried advertising HDS, and gave a few "readings." Hey, you're OK! Look! But no one could understand my excited readings. I gave them my rough impression of the Body Graf and then read each of their twenty-six I Ching Lines—with passion! Waheybi was a religious nut, he used the HDS like a club: "This is you! Don't deny it! I see you!" We made flyers advertising talks on The Human Design System. I walked around town and posted them everywhere. No one came. No one in Boulder was interested, and I didn't know how to advertise. Their cup was full—I understood. We lived in Boulder, after all. But I got frustrated. It became embarrassing to talk about what happened—to me—in Taos. An old time Trungpa follower slapped me violently across the face when I mentioned hearing Trungpa laugh. I can still see my round, gold-rimmed glasses flying across the room to the right. But I had joined the throng of Buddhist students who'd been slapped by a teacher. As a born provocateur, I would have to learn "Strategy And Authority" the hard way. I'd never met a "Generator" in my life. How would I know what "waiting to respond" means?

****

One night at Dance Home, I followed a beautiful young woman onto the dance hall. She walked confidently to the center of the room and sat in a lotus position. I promptly sat facing her. We looked into each other's eyes and it happened. The "fall" into love moment. We enjoyed dancing together and talked after the dance. I asked for her birth information. I still had to make sure my partner was "born again." Everything connected... but left a mental split between us. A mental split can seem OK at first—but wait and see. She moved in with me. I no longer had an income and was in the process of figuring out

133

how I'd survive. Jan worked in the office at the Rolf Institute, just down Pearl St from where we lived. When she left for work, I went on my own adventures. As Ra kept remembering, "stupid before, stupid after." After all, the lust of pornography is but the dark side of resurrection energy! And we'll sure need some cranked-up excitement to overcome the negativity of war, of the enemy! That's what the information said, I-I seemed to be experiencing it all. But I soon wondered, What would it be like to be in a relationship with someone who knows the HDS?

****

Allowing the day to unfold as it would, I found myself on a consistent walkabout. I walked all over Boulder: The Hill (to check on friends), the University for provocations in the square, Naropa Institute for a standing breath-work routine, Pearl St performances, acoustics in the parking garage. I always took a notebook with me to keep a record of my madness. It felt as though I had burst back on stage, no longer watching helplessly from the sidelines. I felt sick of all the shame we carry, sneaking around unworthily! How carefully we walk down the street! Why? I wanted the weird, the alien, the immigrant, the third culture personality to be seen! What did I have to do? Put on a costume? Get tattooed? Why not just dance and sing and shout? What's the worst that can happen—I wanted to know! And I found out.

Waheybi was (still is) a sociopath. Fear of "the crowd" lost its grip on him. He wanted new encounters. Lust was transformed into a raw hunger for any fresh conversation. Lust energy, whether expressed in sex or war or conversation, is never aware, but there will be experience, for good and bad. Every single person struck me as a mystery, yearning to be recognized. But no matter what I did, I still felt invisible. The pressure for self-expression felt overwhelming, and I couldn't contain myself. I wanted to yell, "Hey, something new and wonderful is happening in the world! All this boring self-hatred is not required! You're OK, after all!—there's proof!"

It became impossible for me to sit through any meeting and listen to anyone talk about anything. The aura itself became the playground, the very stage of my theater. To step out of my room was to step onto a stage—all of it, every step! My room was off-stage, but when I stepped out the door, I was on The Stage. The Walkabout Stage! The routine gradually led, naturally, to choreography. When is someone crazy? I didn't think I was crazy, or that I scared people. I wanted to test the social boundaries: when will people react negatively, and to what? I guess that's what crazy is.

So I was walking all over Boulder, going anywhere my interest led me. Someone from Dance Home, who cared for me, suggested that, to be fair, I should wear a costume! She said, "When you go out on the street, you're *acting*—so wear a costume! If you wear normal clothes and perform at the same time, it freaks people out! It's too weird and serious! Put on a costume, a mask, then people are prepared to understand, and leave you alone—you're performing!"

Normalization, the human social rules for blending in with the environment, is just about as thick as cement. If you wobble when you walk, you'll be noticed. If you walk down the street gesturing, it's terrifying for people. When I see someone who walks weirdly, I steer clear of them. The deluded will overwhelm you with their thing. I was too excited for worry and fear. I was on top of the world and just wanted to give away some good news!

****

Anyway, the entire therapeutic community in Boulder came to realize that something strange had happened to Ted. At best, I learned, Ted had an "emergent" experience... but more likely, he had a breakdown. Waheybi was deaf. He couldn't listen to the same boring points of view—and he wanted to talk!—the pressure was too much! He couldn't bear to hear what anyone else had to say, he wanted to "splice the f... movie." But it's impossible to have a normal conversation with someone who reacts emotionally to every word and who fails to listen. It's a miracle, I've learned to fake it, like an alien getting back into his old skin, but with a new angle.

Fools (I'm an Idiot, actually) are really pretty rare. Most of us manage to allow every gesture of the day to follow in conformity with how it's happened before, day to hour to minute, repeating movements—how to walk down the street just so. The whole human world is like a physical hologram with a program for everything. I was somehow breaking through a physical wall made of the space between us. The space is profoundly choreographed. I once encountered my Hakomi teacher, and ex-therapist, who said to me, "You demand too much." It felt as though The Program itself had kicked me out—I would never belong.

It didn't take long for me to settle on a costume. The fool was still in free fall. It wasn't hard to fit the image. A purple jester hat with gold stars and four bells. A white T-shirt with an obnoxious label: "Free New Advice." Bloomer pants with a white background over-laced in newspaper headlines, etc. A large red rain jacket—for the rapidly changing weather in Boulder. And a pair of black wingtip shoes, on plastic bottoms, laced in white wire-style curly laces. A clipboard and notebook. A water bottle, nuts and seeds, a piece of fruit, my weed and a chillum.

Being in the experience of an archetype (the idiot, in my case) is thrilling and frightening. The Boulder Library provided a good place for me to read up on my subject: The Fool—I let the Jester in. On my walkabouts I interviewed random people, asking what they knew about these archetypes. Everyone, I was surprised to learn, has something to say about The Fool and The Jester. In fact, I felt so inspired by my research that I took it to the City Council and petitioned them to pay me for just doing my job. Reporting on my research, I told them, "I seem to meet the requirements for an official Jester, if not The Town Fool. I think you should pay me for my work!" But they all claimed to be fools. Such abject triteness really bugged me, and left me speechless. I walked out still begging for some conversation. A little financial support would have encouraged me.

It so happened that Jan's brother had gone back to his place for lunch that day, and happened, on switching channels, to see me in my outfit—live on Channel 8. That gave him "pause," as they say. Did she not know that she was in a relationship with a crazy person? He called his sister right away to warn her about me.

****

Sunday's were my favorite day for playing Waheybi. Heading straight downtown, I would ask around, "Where can I go to church today? Where can I (my 'not-self' really) be accepted as I am?" The first time I asked, someone suggested I go up to Unity Church, "They'll love you there!" So I walked briskly up Folsom Street and found the Church. The parking lot was packed and the service was well under way, in fact, almost over. As I walked in, the lights were lowered and Jack, the preacher, began to offer a benediction to what must have been a very inspired sermon. Soft music was playing. As I walked down the aisle, there was no available seat. Scanning side to side, I approached the pulpit and stood directly below Jack. He's leaning over the pulpit, eyes closed, intent on his prayer. All I can do is stand there and listen. I start to feel nervous, and an energy rises up from my feet as Jack begins beseeching the Holy Spirit for an anointing. The nervous energy grows, and all I could do was force myself to breathe through it. My arms became wings, pumping up and down, my clipboard and notebook in my right hand, water bottle in my left. As Jack implored the Holy Spirit to descend in power, I had an impression of streams of light raining down through me.

I sobbed and shook under a torrent of energy pouring through. My arms were reaching up to the heavens, I could hardly stand. Tears streamed down my face. The energy subsided even as Jack's prayer came to an end. I finally opened my eyes to see Jack gazing down on me. "Why don't you sit down and wait for the spirit to move," he said... I thought, *wait* for the spirit to move? Now you want me to wait for the spirit to move? Did you not experience the Spirit *moving* just now? I hoped to share my gratitude for the baptism I'd just experienced—under his ministry! They were in a stunned state, and I suddenly realized the experience was designed for me—whatever they experienced—I got it. Perhaps I stammered out something about the air not being real; then re-membered my rule: don't talk till asked. Dummy. Still I burst out and thanked everyone for letting me share in the experience they longed for.

Like walking out of a spaceship into the brilliant sun, I felt deliriously happy and blessed! It was the experience I yearned for in surrender to whatever happens when it does! The streaming, pulsing power of the Spirit rushing through. I always knew there had to be an experience in there somewhere, yet only to be found, after all, in the yearning itself. I could not have imagined a more glorious baptismal moment; the timing was unbelievable, that I would walk in, just then, and receive words as lucent water passing through me from above. Come on!—I thought, that was the baptism for some kind of ministry! But wtf? What was my ministry? Where were my people? None of the religious institutions could, or would, have me. I provoke the hell out of people. That's a dangerous ministry. Is that my ministry? Provoking the hell out of religious people? Out of myself?

****

Jan became absorbed in her own mutative way. She yearned to settle down, to feel supported and safe. Her differentiating process meant she had to find her own way. Her charismatic Generator energy wasn't satisfied. She could no longer waste her energy on other people's business.

Money ran out, and Jan had a miscarriage. It felt, at once, like a tragedy and the "mercy of God." Waheybi was ill-prepared to be a father again; he was too absorbed by the character he played. But Jan suffered. She described it as "shards of glass" tearing through her. That's the worst fantasy. We'd been acting like thirteen-year-old kids. Yet, determined to work through our relational problems, Jan had the bright idea that I would "grow up"—if only I were near my own children in Victoria. "Let's move to Victoria and figure it out!" We had just enough money for a train to Washington State. We didn't know how we'd get to Victoria. We just had to go; another leap into the void.

I knew I was ready for a move when I started parting with my books. I'd stopped reading. I only studied the Rave I Ching, every day, memorizing my Lines. Why would I need to read? The Old Book had been read! It was over! Now I was listening to my own voice as though it wasn't really mine. I didn't know what it might say, but it was interesting! Talk about schizophrenic: The one who talks is not the one who listens.

To be honest, there were some books I still couldn't part with. Gurdjieff's Beelzebub and five volumes of the Philokalia—all the writings of the Desert Fathers. Even these I had to let go. The bookstore owner (in the little town where we stopped in northeast Washington) couldn't give me anything for them. I can see those treasures spread over the counter. Gasp... nothing?? I gave in to the mystical perfection of the moment: to see my valued texts—for nothing.

So we were standing at the train station with our pile of

stuff, but no idea what to do. As we hung out, soaking in our dilemma, we met a local miner who had a little truck. He said he'd be happy to drive us up to the border—and take our stuff! There were boxes of journal writing notebooks full of dreams and dream analysis, a detailed accounting of my sexual history and recovery story, and notes from sessions with therapists. All the years when the war between Jesus and lust took center stage. He said he'd love to read it all, and couldn't wait. We took only what we needed for survival, two backpacks each, and our arms loaded. The Rainbow kids would insist that "you gotta carry all you need in a backpack." So I left the bulk of my past with a miner; he lives somewhere in Idaho.

****

We walked toward British Columbia. As a dual citizen, I had no trouble getting into Canada. My kids live in Victoria. We told the border guard that we were engaged and planned to marry in Victoria. Jan was, by then, upset by my reluctance to marry her. I'd had the marriage experience. Why do it again? But then I started thinking, why not marry? Why not do a Zorba the Greek thing? My Taos experience (ending up in the psyche ward after surrendering to God) became a radical guide, or the iconic example for my path: an experiment in accepting only what's given, what's straight in front of me, in my face. If Jan would stay with me, through this adventure, maybe getting married was… no choice after all.

Once in Victoria, we made our way to the homeless shelter, where I breathed a huge sigh of relief. In a strange way, I was home. My worst fear was fulfilled—the disaster of homelessness. It was like finding an original family, all profoundly interesting human beings! With dread—Jan soon realized—Ted could not provide a stable ground. I was not "growing up" and had more need to play. Something was just beginning. My poor kids never could figure out what happened, or why

I was homeless in Victoria. Where does your Dad live? Your Dad is a homeless person—here in Victoria? When Jan realized I was in no rush to leave Street Link—the homeless shelter in Victoria—she moved over to a protected women's shelter. She then contacted friends in Port Townsend, Washington, and told me that she was going down to "make wedding plans." I was to call her in two weeks.

****

As the ferry pulled away it began to sink in how much I would miss her. And the loneliness was kicking in any way. Being homeless is no joke. You can't quite get over how powerless you feel; I felt as though I existed underneath the sidewalk, looking up at people. People don't realize what an amazing thing it is to have enough money to go into a coffee shop and hang out for hours. You watch people going to work, as though they have something incredibly important to do, glancing at their watches, talking on their phones. The only people who didn't look like manikins were the four-year-old children. Everyone seemed so certain about what they were doing. The only certainty I could verify was hurtling through space, a sort of hybrid neutrino-reading hologram. Or, it was like feeling suspended and going nowhere, no past and no future. Like I didn't have a story or a future.

Two weeks passed and I had to call Jan, so I asked to use the Street Link phone. He said, "Not more than ten minutes."

The first thing she asked me was: "What's your intention?"

"What do you mean—I'm calling to find out how the wedding preparations are going and when I should come down."

Then the bombshell. "Ted, first you need to come back to Jesus, and then you can preach on the streets down here..."

Come back to Jesus? Since when did I ever leave Jesus? I grew up with Jesus! I can't leave Jesus! He is too close to me already!...

"No, you must repent and return to The Lord and then maybe we can talk about our relationship," she said.

I couldn't believe my ears. This Celtic mystic woman, smearing her own menstrual blood on the aspen rod... Come back to Jesus? What is that supposed to mean? She had hooked up with some sort of New Age Christian commune and had a "born again" experience. Groan. I felt sick to my stomach, and knew there was nothing I could do or say about Jesus to change her mind. I hung up the phone and sobbed in front of the Street Link attendant. It felt as though someone I loved had just committed suicide. She had agreed to talk again.

I called her again during the day of Christmas Eve. The person who answered the phone told me that Jan had had a breakdown. Her hair had suddenly fallen out, and now she was in a psyche ward. I felt flung into a state of passion, wrote her a quick poem, and then hopped on the ferry to Port Townsend. I thought it might be easy to find the place, and I had to read her my poem! When I got off the ferry, I discovered that Port Townsend was thirty miles from the ferry! It was Christmas Eve—I hadn't even thought about it. Nothing open but a single little bar. No buses, no cars on the roads; I'd have to walk. So I went into the bar, pounded down a couple of beers and prepared to walk all through the night, if necessary, to find Jan.

As I walked along the road in the pitch dark, I kept calling out her name, as though she might hear me, as though to the Entity, Djah'neen! It was five in the morning, and about ten miles from Port Townsend, when I finally got a ride from another guy in a pickup truck. He dropped me off at a little fish and chips/coffee shop, where I asked the gal behind the counter if she could point me to the hospital that had a psyche ward. She pointed to a road leading up a very steep hill. She thought there was a hospital "just over the hill." I sat down with my coffee and looked at that hill for a while. Maybe it was the exhaustion, but as I gazed, I knew my relationship with Jan was over. It was time to cut my losses and go back home... to the homeless. I promptly hitchhiked back to the Ferry. When I got back to Victoria, I searched for a prostitute, and paid her to listen while I read my poem to Jan.

****

What Jan said about Jesus lit a fire in me. Who is Jesus to me now? Does it matter? Do I really care? I had to find out. So every Sunday I went to three different Church services. The earliest service was at the Anglican Cathedral, where I learned to boom my voice directly into the liturgy. I sang-toned out into the cavernous space from under the stone arches at the entry. The acoustics were great. I also joined their newcomers group, which required a six-month commitment. That was fun, and I did feel welcomed. Then I went over to the Catholic Cathedral—where I ate breakfast every morning, but Sunday. On Sunday, we ate at a place called The Mustard Seed, where we had to endure the preaching before we could eat.

The first time I went to the Catholic Mass, I found myself going up to the front, announcing that I was a new homeless person in town. And, "Since we're all just sitting around here waiting, could I offer a little entertainment before the service begins?" A nice lady called out "sweetie" as she rushed toward me, her hand extended, urging me to "come down from up there!" Returning the next Sunday, I sat calmly in the pews. An usher approached and told me I had to leave and that the police were coming to take me out—if necessary. We walked out to the foyer, where I asked him what the trouble was. He said, "You scare me." And he was shaking. That surprised me. I really didn't want to scare anyone. But I was.

I was stubbornly determined to attend mass the next Sunday... I realized, the only way I could get in would be to join the choir. They had choir practice on Wednesday nights, and they were delighted to have another male voice. It was a thrill, the next Sunday, to walk past the usher as a bonafide choir member. I winked at him and smiled sweetly as I walked past him in my brown painter pant suit, pins and stickers, and up to the front. And the choir loved me. The industrial acoustic voice method I was learning allowed me to sing all the parts, though the baritones provided a safe place to blend in.

****

Perhaps the highlight of my experience in Victoria (besides the utterly amazing people I met) was learning to sing in a new way. A homeless friend had a great suggestion. He said, plug your voice into any persistent hum or buzz, and hone in on the note, the tone. Only when you really have the note, then search for all the harmonies. Sing along with the sounds of the city. He called it "Industrial Acoustics." I came to think of Industrial Acoustics as singing with angels: all the persistent sounds and tones the city provides. If you hone in on those obvious tones, you can sing!—like crazy... all day long! We have angels, what need have we of religion!? We are the homeless and we have our choir masters, the electrical boxes!

There's a big electrical box on the wall by a popular bus stop near the Victoria Library. I could stand inches away from people, tune into the tone and make it boom. I swear they couldn't hear me. I watched them carefully, my mouth as steady as a ventriloquist. My voice would then go wandering into Hindu temples and Islamic prayers. I was constrained by the lesson I learned in a Gurdjieff singing group—the magic in the voice begins with how softly you can sing the note. There is nothing more delightful than to wonder if angels are singing when you can't tell where it's coming from...

Toning in the stairwells of tall buildings, however, provided the most satisfying OMs, and my greatest social challenge. In a tall building, I could be anywhere in the stairwell, and they would have to find me. I'd hear the stairwell doors slamming everywhere, trying to find me somewhere in the forty floors. When they did catch me, the guy told me, "Don't you know, that OM sound goes everywhere, throughout the building, everyone can hear it!?" Then let there be OMing in the stairwells of tall buildings then!

****

The final and thrilling conclusion to my Sunday Church hopping, was to rush over just in time for the fantastic service at Glad Tidings Pentecostal Church. My first meeting there was memorable. The experience made me vulnerable to the delusion, that the gods, or someone was recording my entire experience by secretive means. I was going through something too weird and interesting, for it not to be witnessed. Or was I really alone, a madman. But I also knew these "gods" had only one motive—to be entertained, and never to interfere! Somehow I thought of them as supporting me, but helpless to do anything for me. The more dramatic, and weird, the better—and even better were I to suffer (I say, "God forbid!"). Perhaps I was acting out my "Third Culture Personality Disorder." That's more like it. I have a third culture personality problem.

Anyway, on this particular Sunday, I had slept in and missed the other two services, no doubt due to some sort of late night activity. Perhaps it was a night when the homeless people spent their monthly security check, and later gathered to celebrate the whole night at the beach. Maybe it was the night I danced around the fire and gazed into the Moon, until she was let loose to jiggle in the sky. "Lunatic," I remember a Boulder astrologer calling me—loudly on the street. Anyway, on my way over to Glad Tidings, after a quick toke in a parking garage, I was overcome with a memory of acting in a play in grade two or three in India. I played the part of Artaban, "The Other Wise Man." Part of my role was to sing "O Come O Come Emmanuel" as a solo. I've completely blacked out the memory of the singing, but I can't forget the terror *at the thought of singing the solo.* So now, supported in spirit, I felt a thrilling desire to sing O Come O Come Emmanuel! Hastening on to Glad Tidings, I walked in fashionably late. The place was packed, full of finely dressed, all white, people; and I in my grubby painter coveralls, the front covered in pins, all sorts of stuff.

Homeless people wear uniforms. When I landed at Street Link, in my ordinary guy clothes, a kid I'd befriended instructed me on the necessity of wearing a proper "homeless person uniform." You have to dress for the street, he said. A store next to Street Link sold cheap or free clothing. So he took me over there and recommended my daily uniform. A quality brown bag coveralls with an obvious brass zipper down the front. In the summer I would cut the legs down from the hips to about six inches from the bottom, offering a lovely clown-like impression, my legs billowing along in the flutter of the strands. Another nice feature of the coveralls was the art I made of pins, buttons and stitchery. I wore a beige tuque on my head. A simple white towel from the hotel made an excellent scarf. A towel, string, and a little knife are requirements for street living.

So, as I slowly walked down the center aisle it became apparent that the only seat available was at the very front row on the left. A spectacular single beam of sunlight shone directly on the seat. Either the gods were on my side, or seducing me once again. Having reached the very front seat, I became aware of the vast open space between me and the pastoral team and, behind them, a huge choir.

Someone right behind me, kindly, slid a hymn book into my hands, and conveniently opened it to the hymn they were all singing. I've forgotten the title of the hymn now, but after not more than a stanza or two, I noticed a phrase coming up: "prophets of old." I was gripped with a pounding sense of inevitability. Sure enough, as the words were sung, I whirled around in unison, slamming the book shut in my raised hands and shouted at the top of my lungs, "Prophets Of Old-dah!"

When I had first turned to face the crowd, they all had their faces buried in their hymn books, but when I shouted, suddenly, their heads and eyes snapped up, leaving the impression of a wind suddenly stirring up dust. It was a clear impression, though it was mean of me. A little boy yelling boo from out of a bush. Nevertheless, I turned back to the front and composed myself, thumbing through the Hymn book, looking for the song.

As I was doing so, an usher came up on my right and asked me, "Can you keep it down."

I said, "Yes, I'm fine, let's carry on..." or some such. But he didn't move away and kept standing there, facing me from the aisle.

Finally I turned to him and pressed my left hand into his chest, over his striped tie, and said, "Brother, if you've come here to worship God today, do so with me, it's why I came!" That's just what I said.

Then I noticed the Pastor walking toward me from the elevated area, and as he approached, he was gazing at the bobby pins, etc., on my coveralls, not looking into my face at all. Like, what's all that weird stuff on your coveralls? So I used my two fingers in the "look at me" gesture and got him to raise his eyes to mine.

I promptly shared the memory I'd had walking over to Glad Tidings, that I was a missionaries' kid from India, and how, when I was in grade two had played the part of Artaban, "The Other Wise Man." "I had to sing a solo, 'O Come O Come Emmanuel,' but Pastor, I couldn't have felt more terrified, then, and I don't remember singing the song. But now I feel the urge to sing. Please let us sing that song today."

As I was sharing this memory with the Pastor, I felt calming hands on my shoulders and sliding gently down my arms. It felt pleasurable and harmless; I hardly paid attention; I was so absorbed in my story. Actually, there were two men touching me, and a few standing ready. Before I could think twice, one of the men took the pinky of my right hand, and the other took the index finger of my left hand.

Simultaneously, and with perfect timing, they slammed the pinky of my right hand into my sternum and my left index finger up to a point high between my shoulder blades. My first thought, surprisingly, was the professional quality of a police tactic—this was the most efficient way of moving someone in my condition. To resist—at all—would break my fingers. My second thought was quite absurd, and involved a feeling of identification with Jesus; but in a way I hadn't anticipated. As I was being dragged down the aisle, it occurred to me that Jesus had been thrown out of the Synagogue, having provoked his own people. Here's a missionaries' kid, at Glad Tidings Pentecostal Church shouting "prophets of old," and being thrown out!

It can happen! It was actually happening to me! The difference between me and Jesus was that He could disappear: I was not going to get away so easily. But pain has a way of opening the stops when there's nothing left to lose. So I yelled again, "You don't have to hurt me!"

When they reached the front door, the brother with the firm grip on the arm behind my back, literally kicked the door open and unceremoniously dumped me to the ground on my side. As they did so, one of them stooped down at me and, in a hushed and fierce tone, said, "Go get some treatment!" Whereon I lunged back toward the closing door and, before it shut, shouted loudly through the crack, "The Romans are still in charge here!"

Madness. I scared people, and that's not a nice thing to do. People get scared very easily, as I was finding out. It was becoming clear to me, in my sociopathic state, in my determination to explore my new relationship with the world, that I was ignoring the fact that we humans, our bodies, are actually suspended in a state of fear. It's the very frequency of fear that allows the body to have existential awareness. Ironically, the famous "now"—we speak of as "enlightenment"—is a *state of fear!* So, what people really need is gentleness and understanding. It makes no sense to scare people when they are already afraid.

But Waheybi was more like a kid who'd forgotten what it's like when someone jumps out and yells, "Boo!" It's not fair, I know. I remember how I didn't like it when people did that to me... made me want to kill something—quick. It's a dangerous thing to do, as I was finding out at a whole new level.

****

The experience at Glad Tidings threw my emotional system into overdrive. I didn't know what to do with the energy. I felt something coming through my skin from the inside, and I couldn't jump up and down enough, or dance it off. On the one hand, there was the simple excitement, that I was alive in the world. I felt as though the people around me should understand the momentous nature of the times; like it was time to announce the apocalypse: "Finally!—We're Here!"

The energy had the feel of a mad whirling dance, but I hadn't whirled—yet. Now, suddenly, I knew what to do. That afternoon, I ran down to the beach from my hotel room, found an open grassy area and started to run in a circle, closer and closer to a spin, until I felt out of control. Wrestling with suicidal energy, I pressed my body faster, closer to the point on the front ball of the foot. But as I reached the top of my capacity, running in circles to catch the spin, I knew I couldn't stop or I'd stumble and fall. An inner voice said calmly, distinctly, "Try just slowing down a little." By easing up on the gas, I found that slowing down was possible. When I finally came to a standstill, I saw something I'd never seen before, and haven't seen since: I saw the earth and sky as separate, my eye fixed on the flat plane of the horizon flying past. There were no visual details, just the constant flow of the horizon, earth and sky in a blur of motion before my eyes. I stood perfectly still for a long time, watching heaven and earth fly past me from right to left, wondering what would happen if it didn't stop. I never got dizzy again. Although a friend once gave me some mushrooms... but that's a different story.

****

I really didn't think I'd stay homeless forever, so I consciously embraced my day-to-day experience and tried to be a good student of homelessness. My first lesson came from a more jaded homeless friend. He reacted to my tendency for "telling" and "intellectualizing"—as though I were *not* "just another fucked up homeless person." This was blatantly true. I've never lost the sense of being an "almost retarded" school kid. Now I felt like someone who had finally learned something—and because I am not very smart, everyone should know what had—finally—become obvious to me! But with homeless people, no appeal to education and highfalutin language means anything. Many of them *are indeed* highly educated, and further educated by painful life experiences.

I met more genius types, or at least more interesting people on the street, than I've ever met in "normal" settings. Normality constrains any expression of uniqueness. Many homeless people have such a unique view of life and experience, but have never been able to communicate it clearly. They become "freaks," often ranting their unique point of view—to the grave: voices in the wilderness, I tell you. Some homeless people have had experiences, as I had, which render them unable to negotiate the nine-to-five workday world. They need time to process what's happened to them.

Some of my homeless friends came from backgrounds that boggled my mind. My friend Andrew was the sweetest guy.

Really smart. He'd been adopted by a rich couple who treated him worse than an animal you wanted to kill, slowly. No one knew about his plight. They kept him in a room for years, feeding him animal food and crackers, while they ate high off the hog in the next room. He often didn't get water for days, and regularly drank his own urine three times over. I think social services finally caught up to those people. Sometimes, I think white Americans, in their separate homes, hide the weirdest, if not abusive, conditions on the planet. But Andrew could speng up five dollars in no time.

****

I had made a real effort to learn how to speng. In fact, at first, I thought maybe I'd finally found a job that suited me. So I interviewed the other regular spengers. They gave me great advice. Treat it like a regular job. Find a place, claim your territory, and always go back to the same spot. Be disciplined— show up. Take breaks. Smile and be friendly because the customer is always right. But I just couldn't do it. I couldn't sit in one spot all day—no way. There was too much wandering around to do, too many adventures to have. And I couldn't take the chronic rejections, and I didn't have the patience. It hurt too much to feel the abjection of being homeless, just sitting there on the side of the street, people literally looking down on you.

Anyway, right after breakfast at the Catholic Cathedral, Andrew would speng up enough for our first joint for the day. A small group of us walked down to the park near the beach for conversation, talking like crazy... exploring all kinds of ideas. Then I'd go to the Library atrium and sing. When I sang in the atrium at night, one of the guards would get angry and drive me away.

Running just ahead of him, I turned to ask him, "Why do you keep chasing me off?"

151

He said, in a strong British accent, his face all puffy and red, "You know very well; it's all moaning, groaning and drivel!"

I remember it exactly: moaning, groaning and drivel. If I ever record an album, that's what I'll call it: "Moaning, Groaning, and Drivel." Maybe a three-piece band.

A few of the drunks were actively drinking themselves to death. I knew three of them—in those nine months—who did just that. I watched them, every day, drink themselves to death. It's a profound relief to discover amorality toward such human behavior. I took notes of their experience. Perhaps that was my grief, that they were not somehow recording their experience; that such rich experience was being wasted. Every homeless person's story is worthy of a movie. Like every "criminal" story is. It's as though the whole human journey gets compressed into the problems of a homeless person. Without a story, including therapy—to encompass, and share, the experience—we never learn! We never learn a thing about crime when the end result is jail—as though justice is done! Every human being expresses something universal about the human condition! And yet, how overlooked somehow, how wasted? The problems we experience provide a way to recognize the parallel with global problems everywhere! Your conflicts are not yours. For example, We all exist in some zone between the Jews and the Palestinians. Which one are you—when you argue with your girlfriend, or your wife? Or the people you work with? Or...its endless.

****

There was a famous Chinese homeless guy; they called him "Professor." He never spoke to anyone, so all we knew was a legend. A chemistry professor and an experiment that went wrong. There was no way you could get him to talk. On one occasion, however, walking past him after breakfast, as he leaned against a wall, I heard him mumble something to me, when I knew no one else could have heard. Thereafter, I thought of his silence as a best defense against the world. It seemed at times that we could recognize each other from across the room. It was spooky, but I thought he was OK with me, and I found him intriguing. He wore black ladies' high heels. His hair was straight down and cut at odd, pointed angles. He buttoned his shirt unevenly, which seemed deliberate to me. I'd often see him walk out into the middle of the street and stoop to pick up some tiny object. Then he would stand there and examine it, completely absorbed, oblivious (it seemed) to the traffic.

Christopher, another homeless guy, became a friend. He sang on the street and wore a long black trench coat. He had the loudest singing voice I have ever heard. He let me sing with him. But Christopher was suicidal. One evening he came to see me at the Douglas Hotel. I had graduated from Street Link and was provided a room just above the door to the Karaoke bar.

Every morning at about 2 AM, I would rush to the window and watch the drunks argue and beat each other up. It annoyed me, that I was so interested—the way a drunk head will twist around when punched. Anyway, I was sitting there in the coffee shop writing, when in comes Christopher, drenched from the rain. He sits down and tells me that he had a dream the night before of meeting Jesus in a coffee shop. He confessed to Jesus that he was suicidal, but Jesus couldn't help him. I told him I was a Muslim, which is true. I had begun to hear Islamic chants in my head and had found out that the random name I chose for myself, Waheybi, sounded too much like the most radical branch of Islam, the Wahhabis! And a few days before, while walking down the street, I had heard inwardly, distinctly, another name for myself: Zaman!

That sent chills through my body. Who is Zaman? I met an Iranian woman in the Library and asked her if Zaman meant anything to her. She said that in Iran it was another name for

The Mahdi. I had only been to the Mosque twice, but they informed me, that because I had simply said "the prayer," that I was now a Muslim. A brother from the Mosque saw me on the street, spenging and singing with Christopher and gave me twenty dollars. I commented on the extravagance, but he was adamant that it was merely his duty as a Muslim brother to help me however he could. With the voices in my head, and the urge to scream Allah u Akbar at the top of my lungs, I felt nervous about identifying myself as a Muslim. I thought I should stop trying to further that connection. But not until after an experience of shouting Allah u Akbar in the mall—as loudly as I could.

I had learned how the downtown Mall in Victoria is actually built in the geometry of a Mosque. I had no idea, but it sounded right to me. Well, that tweaked my budding and ignorant zeal for Islam. For a few days I explored where the best place would be to shout Allah u Akbar three times, as loudly as I could—and get away with it! If the place was built like a Mosque, then it needed a proper dedication. It just had to be done. I took off my shoes and stood at the railing, calling Allah u Akbar three times into the space so that everyone in the whole Mall would hear. In seconds, the guards ran at me from all directions, surrounding me. That was before the Twin Towers came down, or I might not be alive today. Anyway, I have the feeling that someday I'll have to find out what it means to be a Muslim.

Anyway, you can't just tell a suicidal person to "have a nice day." I had just met a young couple who were freshly zealous for reading The Bible. The guy was another delusional person who identified somehow with Jesus, so it was good timing for me to take Christopher over there. I knew they would have to take him in. They loved nothing better than to get stoned, or tripped out on other drugs, and read the Bible. I guess a lot of people find the Bible quite interesting when they're tripping. I couldn't get into it, but if Christopher was talking about Jesus, I thought they would be the best people for him to be with. I didn't hear anything for three days. Hoping Christopher was OK, I was waiting for dinner at Street Link, standing in line, when my Jesus friend approached to tell me that Christopher had jumped off the bridge. He'd been rescued downriver but died from hypothermia three days later. I've never burst so suddenly into tears as I did then, covering my face with my hands. He was in the hospital for three days, and I didn't know about it.

****

During the last two months in Victoria, I actually had a girlfriend, of sorts. We had a very light and friendly relationship. I treated her like a virgin. She was a young woman from Quebec who worked as a dealer at a casino and stripper club. She seemed so innocent to me, and was just learning to speak English. Then Don called to say that I had a job waiting for me in Boulder, should I want to return. It so happened that Dad and Elizabeth were traveling down through the States again, and could give me a ride all the way to Boulder. As I was running down the street to meet them at the ferry, I accidentally passed my French speaking friend and told her, with some excitement, that I had a chance to return to Boulder. Heartless bastard. She started wailing, brokenhearted. She made me realize, as though I hadn't known it before, that there is always a risk when a woman opens her heart to you. But I was programmed to run.

****

Chief Niwot once cursed Boulder. The Indians used the area strictly for sacred ceremony. No one actually lived in Boulder. It would have been like living in the temple or the church—you just don't do that. So when the white man kept moving

155

in, and there was no stopping them, he cursed the place. He said that people who lived there, and moved away would have to return. There was another part to the curse that fascinated me. This is my understanding of it. He suggested, because Boulder is a spiritual area, and not a place to live, that those who continued to live there would become so spiritually fat they would implode.

13

Out With The Old...

Back in Boulder; I was off the street but continued to wear my street clothes, my hair in a messy dread knot down the back of my head. I moved in with Don, who was living as an overnight caregiver for a dying old alcoholic named Blackie. Blackie had daytime caregivers, so Don and I were only required for night duty, and to make sure he got his breakfast before the other caregivers arrived in the morning.

After my own breakfast, I found a place to smoke a joint, readying myself for the evolving Walkabout. From aimless wandering, the routine had changed and synthesized to essential elements that could be repeated like any yoga practice. The environment had disciplined me into keeping my talking tongue tied. No more random shoutouts—"There is no universe, it's all an Entity inside Mama!" Every step of the way was choreographed for dance and song and theater, all oriented around the breath—I was learning to fly. The Fool's outfit and the street clothes no longer felt appropriate; still, a uniform was required.

A routine, no matter how outrageous (now within the boundaries I had learned from experience), gave people a chance to accept my unique expressions of individuality, of theater. From behind the costume, I was free to perform. A friend of mine, who lived on the grounds of the Hanuman Temple in Taos, had given me an orange hat with the Sanskrit

"Ram" emblazoned on it. "Hare Krishna Hare Ram, Rama Rama, Hare Hare..." The color orange suggested (to me at the time) the vocation of a monk engaged in holy action. Perhaps I was a fool, but hopefully perceived as a "holy fool," or an expression of "crazy wisdom." Hu knows.

And the walkabout practice *was* increasingly satisfying. I had found something totally satisfying in my experience, and that I could practice and improve on endlessly. In fact, I wouldn't have believed how tolerant people can be. I just had to behave! As long as I just whirled and used sign language, no one interfered. Perhaps I was developing an art-form for those mad souls who can no longer keep silent, or march in step with "hometown."

Where, in the beginning, I had hoped for interaction with the public, I learned through practice, though still motivated "to save the world" (5th Line theme), was actually support for my own emotional development. It was my honest expression, and it was also a real performance. I was not showing off. I was showing up. The uniform and unusual behavior created a protective aura for the unique art form. What should I call it? Diogenes?

So here's the practice I did, and still do, in different settings. I began with an OM in the tunnel under Pearl St. at the west end of Boulder. Tunnels are made for toning. Then, running down the bike path, I whirled and danced across the grass behind the Justice Center (which looks like a fortress—for me to challenge). The whirling non-verbal sign language routine was based on the ten stages of the Prenatal Sequence. Determined to simplify each stage/center/religion, I learned to say each category in sign language. (These ideas were presented in my first book, The Gathering Dogma!) Here's the simplified version, easy to say in Sign Language and powerful to express in whirling and dance:

Welcome Home Friend.
Listen We say Be here...

Now, to gather In stillness breathing The innocent
child everything is...
Awake!

Running further down the Boulder Creek Path, I acknowl-
edged the statue of Chief Niwot and kissed his feet, then
sprinted as fast as I could toward the lawn in front of the
Boulder Public Library. There I sang, while whirling, the
Welcome Home... Song. I wanted everyone in Boulder to hear
it, as a mantra, and never with additional commentary. People
would accept my loud singing as long as I stuck precisely to
the formula and resisted all impulses to continue with commentary. My practice became a regular part of the Boulder
scene, like "This is a warning system test..." proclaimed every
Monday morning over a very powerful loudspeaker system.
When things happen like clockwork, people dismiss it (quickly)
thanks to the marvel of our reticular activating system.

There's a happy section on the Pearl St Mall that's blocked
to traffic. Street performers galore: magical acts, jugglers, all
kinds of singers, poets and preachers, another mad guy in a
Viking outfit—horns and all. I would dance/whirl/sign my
way through the entire length of the mall, with a special performance, integrated with the stonework geometry in front of
the Court House. There I whirled in, swooping to the ground
in a gesture of rescuing and exalting a baby. In fact the dance
involved a series of extreme dance forms and gestures: tumbling across the lawn, flying with The Eagle, landing on a walk-
way, spinning through a series of obstacles on the way toward
the door of the Courthouse. Waheybi was occasionally questioned by the police, and others. But he wasn't drunk, or dangerous. What could they do? Though Waheybi really wanted
to shout—in commentary—he'd been consistently punished
for bursting out. The satisfying experience, he really wanted,
he found in the wisdom of silence and gesture, not in shouting and then having to deal with reactions. This lesson saved

me, I'm sure of it. I had no idea how much protection and power there is—available in following Strategy and Authority. So the practice became deep and strong and confident—but contingent on resisting the temptation to speak out.

Street preachers gave me a reason to break my "no talking" rule. Who has not heard them shouting out your personal "sin:" "lasciviousness?" Such talk now can ignite my adrenaline system, a bristle up my spine like a call to battle. They gave me license to approach and stand beside them, adjusting my voice, via industrial acoustics, in harmony with the tone of the preacher's voice. It's as though you were listening to a voice on the radio, and suddenly another channel begins breaking in on the same frequency, in harmony.

Why do we stand and listen while someone tells us how bad we are, and threatens us with eternal torture? Unless it's really StandUp comedy—that's what Ra called it. There must be such a blanket of shame-blame-guilt over us, that we tolerate such rhetoric in public! It's hardly an evolution from the public torture and disembowelment spectacles of the Middle Ages. Repulsed by the condemning language I'd heard as a child, I countered it with: "You are all innocently ignorant! This man is having a nightmare, and though I am joined with him in the nightmare, it is my responsibility to hear a different message. I don't need that message any more, so I'm going to throw in my voice with a commentary song. You can listen along, we'll be in harmony. I'll reject the blaming rhetoric placed on the physical- individual-scapegoats. The enemy I kill is under the dome of my skull...." At which point the preacher would confirm my viewpoint on "the nightmare" and start casting out demons. Undeterred, I persisted along with him, until the dude quit preaching and got off his soap box. There are times, after all, for an open throated assault on negativity.

When there were no preachers, I spun and danced and signed my way down to the east end of the Mall. Just east of the mall was a parking garage with wonderful acoustics in the basement. A great place for singing the Welcome Home song, but now in their original sounds, those signature acoustic secrets—for each religion. Having abandoned all religious practice (to find my own), I wanted to rescue the essential sounds for each of the ten religions of the world. Following the logic of the ten Stages of the Prenatal Sequence (plotting out the ten religions), I searched for each essential sound. Perhaps you could improve on it—but you'll have to prove it. This is an acoustic formula, expressing the range of Homo Religious! Sacred sounds. Hear the magic of Religion, this My Dogma Song—Sing Yours—Along!

Eiyahua (eleven times, the last a nice shout)

Silence

Kyria... hare hare.

Six Alleluias with an

Allah u Akbar on the third.

The Native Cry Ya Heyya heyheyya heyheyya... Hey.

The six Taoist sounds Sii... Whhh... Shhh... HAAA... HOOO... HRIII (firm jaw on the last).

Welcome Home Friend. Listen, We Say Be Here Now To-Gather In Stillness Breathing Djah'neen Is Awake! (The religious synthesis).

The Russian Orthodox Gospodi Pomilui and the name of the Unborn Entity, Djah'neen.

Ending with the Buddhist tones: Om, Ong, Hung, Ha, Ho, Hrii.

They tried to stop me from singing in the parking garage. For the first few months of my practice, a security guard or officer told me, three or four times, that I could be heard throughout the building, then reiterating that they were merely messengers. So I'd respond, "Then be a good messenger and send a message back: Expect this! Once or twice a week, there will be five minutes of chanting down here."

Sometimes, a female police officer would come down and

stand at a distance. Or, perhaps to discourage me, a guard would arrive and park close by with the engine running. Ah, what the angels do to get us to sing—raise the pitch! Eventually, they quit trying to stop me. And I accepted it as a grace, and motivation always to sound better and better, higher and lower and louder and softer, more undeniably beautiful, if haunting. In seven years, I never heard a single complaint. In fact, the opposite.

****

Waheybi had lost all sense of meaningful practice for religious engagement. His way was the way of emotional openness and chaos, of going out and getting into trouble, of finding out what worked and didn't work, exploring the extremes. Live music and dancing, however, provided all the meaning Waheybi could have asked for in the world. According to Waheybi (the performer), "Heaven is a live band, a dance floor, and an audience full of uptight white people." As so often happens in America, in "caucasian culture" especially, one can witness a great band, playing—eminently danceable music—and no one dancing but children!

It was in the context of the summer "Concerts In The Park" where Waheybi discovered his favorite spiritual discipline, a form and a context where he could express his thoughts and feelings with abandon. I highly recommend the practice for anyone merely brave enough. The Band Shell in Boulder was his favorite venue. Imagine a band playing under the Band Shell, an open dance area and a few children running around. The band has already played a few songs, and there are still no adults on the dance floor. And then appears a guy wearing an orange T-shirt and orange Ram cap. It doesn't take long before he rolls around on the gravel dance floor and spins wildly, gesturing in some kind of sign language.

Hey, in whatever form, people always appreciate and enjoy

the expression of talent. They can respect someone who spins around and doesn't fall. He might appear to be crazy (so you stay back), but his movements are uncanny. When he gestures, you can almost understand him. He creeps into your mind. The experience of whirling-in-sign-language provided a way for me to share an inner journey through the logic of Sequencing, inspired by the music and expressed in dance. Delusions are handy for the performance artist. One must be abandoned to the experience and identified (without being identified) with the expression. I'm grateful for places like City Park Jazz in Denver, Rhythm on the Rails in Niwot, the Boulder Band Shell, and Band on The Bricks. The gift of tolerance, that humans have for art—and I felt deeply—allows for self-acceptance and empowerment in the performer. When my art was not accepted, I did feel humiliated, but I think that only happened when I had failed to follow my Strategy and Authority, like bursting out to talk when no-one had asked.

****

Something else had changed: lust, seemingly, evaporated. When I resumed my attendance at Sex Addicts Anonymous meetings, I had the awful feeling of being at Church again, or in a class—and wanting to quit. My experience of lust had been transformed from an inward oppression to the excitement of penetrating the human aura with dance, song, and theater. I could no longer look at a woman to objectify her sexually; what I really wanted was friendly connection and sharing, more of a seduction around seeing the whole world in a new way. Sick of the focus on sin, fixing problems, self-improvement, my whole life seemed to have been focused on: what's wrong with me!—how can I change myself? Self improvement... yuk... Now I loved my messy character! The thought of *continuing* to review my past and outline my shortcomings, felt too oppressive.

In a rambunctious mood, I went to a meeting and announced myself as a graduate of the twelve-step program. Unthinkable. A sensitive newcomer walked out in protest; an old timer brought him back. I'd been a core member, among those who hung out for the coffee-after meeting. It was the last thing they wanted to hear: "Once an addict, always an addict." Now, I'm not saying my sexual obsessions won't come back. Who knows, lust may return with a vengeance in my old age. But for the time being, I just didn't experience lust as a problem. I had come to the conclusion that people who need the twelve-step program, as a religion, are simply the ones who need it. Someone who drinks a lot, and has no desire to quit, or change, is not an "Alcoholic." When human beings do things that hurt other people, as a result of some compulsive behavior, that can be a sign of a need for intervention and therapy, but they have to want help. Thank God—I say—for the twelve-step program! It saved my life at a time when I truly needed that support. But now I was having too much fun, as Waheybi, to be reminded of sins and addictions and shortcomings. I was still plunging headlong into a new experience, paying my dues in a new exchange. Waheybi has had no time to reflect on the problems of the past; he was (and will always be) too young and futuristic.

****

Blackie's health deteriorated rapidly. He seemed to enjoy my presence and took full advantage of my weaknesses as a caregiver. Every single morning, for example, he would get up from the recliner, on which he slept, and leave plops of wet shit on the hallway carpet all the way to the bathroom. I cleaned it up with the demeanor of someone gathering flowers. He loved my attitude, and the massages I gave him on his recliner. We enjoyed long talks, often centered on his crazy experiences with booze and womanizing.

On one of my daily walkabouts, I met a traveling hippy named Wey. Ji Wey had lived in India a few times, seemed enlightened, and looked exactly like my Jesus. He didn't resist the equation; and I didn't mind giving it to him, or anyone who wanted to play Jesus. Since I was feeling identified with Muhammad (pbuh), and after training my mind with ACIM, I determined to see everyone (in my mind) as Jesus in the flesh; and if someone really was identified with Jesus—what entertainment! Now, let's get down to work! After all, only the deluded can change the world!

Wey had recently inherited a pile of money from his deceased parents, and expressed a wish to take me back to India with him. How could I refuse? Of course! Take me! When can we go? Wey then left Boulder, taking care of some business, and bought a camper van in San Francisco. There was something he wanted me to experience before leaving for India: "You must meet *your people* at The Rainbow Gathering in Montana." I didn't know what to think, but it sounded exciting, so I waited for his call.

Meanwhile, Don and I had discovered a few people in Boulder who had also met Ra Uru Hu, and who were interested in forming a group to study the Human Design System. Six or seven of us met in the comfortable basement at Blackie's townhouse. That's where I met Anne: sweet, generous, long-suffering Anne. We became friends, and enjoyed talking about The Human Design System. When I told her of my "India plan," she invited me—in preparation for my trip—to stay at her house on Retreat. The thought of such leisure was irresistible. But this left Don with Blackie—and Don does not clean up shit. No way. He told Blackie, in no uncertain terms, "I know Ted cleaned up your shit, but I won't do it." Blackie promptly quit shitting his way to the bathroom! I felt miffed, I couldn't believe it. What kind of science/miracle/magic trick can do that? Was he taking advantage of me? Was it consciously done? Was it a healing experience for him—to be cared for like

165

that? Was it the nature of our electromagnetic connection? Human Design suggested that he was, in fact, innocent in his true hypocrisy, which helped me get the joke. The not self-mind loves to judge; the correct explanation is acceptance. Understanding can be funny.

****

I moved in with Anne and used the month as a Lunar retreat, tracking the journey of the moon through the sixty-four hexagrams of the I Ching. So by "meeting" The Moon at the very minute, day or night, when she entered a gate (one of sixty-four Hexagrams), even if it was 2:03 AM, I could write out my own copy of The Rave I Ching. It would have been easy to photocopy the material, but I wanted to physically write down the six I Ching Lines, and Ra's commentary, called "The White Book." By the end of the month, I had my own Rave I Ching and would do this once a year for the next three years. Eventually, I invented my own version of The I Ching. Pithy little things.

At the end of the month, Wey was ready for our journey to The Rainbow Gathering in Montana. Montana 2000, my first Rainbow Gathering! During my month on retreat with Anne, Wey had gone to San Francisco and purchased a nice little camper truck. He asked me to meet him in SF, drive up the coast to Washington and across to Montana. He paid for my airfare. The whole experience changed my life, and gave me a new sense of "religion." I'd never been so excited before, as though I were on my way to the Promised Land! Perhaps the most exciting thing about The Gathering is the moment of decision—to "Go!" There is something mystical/magical in the very act of "going" and traveling to The Gathering. The Gathering begins, in fact, when you leave where you are—and go!

As we traveled, Wey told me about The Rainbow Gathering. It all sounded to me like the last stand of the '60's. The first

Gathering was held in 1972, just down the road from Boulder, near Red Rocks. Some hippy had had a vision, where Jesus came to him, like Kevin Costner in the movie, "Field Of Dreams:" "If you build it, they will come." A hippy commune from New York was in on it, and moved to the Boulder area in an attempt to escape New York City. Then there were "The Kids" who followed The Grateful Dead—with their dogs. The "Kitchens"—so central to the hippy experience in San Francisco—was essential. The Antiwar Movement. Vietnam vets who've learned to live in the woods—all across the Americas. The Gathering subsumed the spirit of the '60's: freedom of the individual, peace and love; and of course, the use of pot and LSD and magic mushrooms—natural stuff—other drugs were discouraged, but hey. Drugs and Alcohol are really Tribal problems, and best dealt with Tribally. The local Native Indian Tribal Authority, inherent in the establishment of the site, provided a spiritual orientation for the entire Gathering.

You can survive at the Gathering without money, because everyone brings an abundance, for sharing, and for the Trade Circle. The Gathering is a voice in the wilderness (so it may not be heard) for a global permaculture economy. Everyone who came to The Gathering was expected to bring extra food and camping gear, gems and jewelry, extra clothes, like wool socks, also rope, tarps, and a good knife. And the setting had to be perfect, as paradisiacal as could be: meadows and woods and a stream with a source for drinkable water. It had to be accessible by forest roads, yet many miles from the nearest town. And there had to be a huge area suitable for parking.

The one thing that really bugged Wey was the drunks at A Camp. He didn't like alcohol anywhere near The Gathering. In the beginning, "A Camp" was simply "a camp"—where The Gathering initially met. Then the drunks became such a huge problem (quick to destroy the "peace and love" commitment!) that the "Main" Gathering was moved to a location requiring a three to five-mile trek through the woods. Drunks generally don't plan to walk through the woods in the dark. They normally want a direct experience with other human beings. Park-n-party.

The three, big problems/issues for The Gathering, I discovered, were: 1) keeping the alcohol limited to A Camp, along with threats of violence; 2) what is needed in taming the spirit of A Camp, but Dance, Song, and Theater—Company; 3) and the dogs (to leash or unleash): an inner tribal gathering where dogs are unleashed, a mesoteric civilized gathering area where the dogs are leashed, and A Camp, the external Gathering, the interface with Babylon—and chaos.

So we know that drinking alcohol lowers something in humans called GABA, which inhibits certain social behaviors. Drunks just are vulnerable to all sorts of excitement, aggression, and oppressive memories. This is both good and bad. In the end I'd conclude that The Gathering is like a microcosm of the world—with all our hopes and fears crunched into a single location. And A Camp is a burning hot spot. It really is mundane; it's what humans do, and emotions can be expressed! Perhaps a dance/song/theater Company/Army may contain it?

Another factor joining The World to The Gathering, was the presence of Law Enforcement Officers (LEOs). You don't have to go to Israel to struggle for Peace on Earth—just go to a Rainbow Gathering. The US government, from the first Gathering in 1972, organized a branch of government for dealing with the new movement, infiltrating, disrupting, and marching through with guns. We were all to be on alert for the LEO's and yell "Six Up," as an alarm whenever we spotted them. I advocated for the idea that "Six Up" become an occasion for rushing into a dance, song, and theater practice! What better way to escort the warmongering through sacred Earth!

The Tribal/State human boundary has never been easy, and it's problematic by Design. I think we're here to figure it out. We, so far, have no bridge between the heart (The Tribe, Islam) and the sacral center (The Capitalist and the Permaculturist), between the LEO's and The Rainbow. I wondered, as an experiment, could I experience The Rainbow Gathering as a microcosm of what's going on between The Jews and The Palestinians? The micro/macro principle is really useful as a perspective on all my interpersonal problems. It gives my little problems a big view.

As soon as we reached Seed Camp, Wey banished me from the camper, along with the illusion of ease in daily living. I had a tent, a sleeping bag, and a couple of pairs of clothes. He yelled at me as I walked away, "You're at The Rainbow Gathering now, you'll survive!" We were in the woods for a whole month before the official start of The Gathering on July 1st—when the general public arrive in droves. We ate strictly potato and onion for two weeks. While traveling with Wey, I had become addicted to the peanut butter and jam sandwich. After three days of potato—you crave one of those.

If you've ever been in the woods at night, you know how easy it is to get lost. Every year I go to the Gathering and get lost—at least once—stumbling around all night with no sense of direction. Fortunately, as more hippies arrive, there are more fires to serve as guides. With every fire I stumbled on, I found new friends, like old friends. Friends and coffee, drums and conversation. However, stumbling around in the dark (I resolutely refused to use a flashlight), it was easy to fall into a shitter. In fact, The Rainbow Gathering invented the term "Shit Happens."

As for meaning, one of my favorite experiences of The Gathering is lying in my tent at night listening to the various drum circles move in and out of sync. When those drums get going, and in sync, you feel exhilaration in the liquid of the cells. What is a "culture" without public drumming?

What impressed me the most about The Gathering was the friendly spirit I felt. I still romanticize my early impressions, and though my returns to the Gathering have brought challenges, I still maintain a kind of religious belief, even faith, in the hope of The Rainbow Gathering. Can anyone really stomach what's happening in Israel today? What a sick story—

unless it's about "the lost kids" at the Rainbow Gathering! The Rainbow Gathering does not wait—it's happening all the time now. We are performing human hope. We are the experience of religious completion! What is there to do but... The Rainbow Gathering in Israel!

The Kids call the world—beyond The Gathering—"Babylon." They called me an "elder." After being homeless, and my experience of madness, I was amazed to discover the value they gave to my experience and my words. In Babylon, I was merely crazy, my experience literally worse than useless, unwanted— you're a sex addict, a psychopath, a sociopath, a lunatic, a religious nutcase, and something happened to you that makes no sense to any of us. But I thought The Kids respected me, and tried to show it. I wasn't (just) a crazy person. Au contraire, my voice was actually sought for, and needed.

Over the years, I'd come to know some of the homeless people in the Boulder area, and then I'd see them at The Gathering—like stars. They were suddenly transformed in my eyes into icons of beauty and wisdom; from the Boulder lowlifes as I had seen them on the city street. The shift in my perspective, and the powerful conditioning of context, was remarkable to me.

****

While it's true that I felt respected by the white hippy kids at The Gathering, it was two Muslim brothers, Omar and Muhammad, who made me feel, not just like an elder but like an Imam... or Rabbi, or something. And before I say more about Muhammad and Omar, I must first tell you the story of my first encounter with The Jerusalem Kitchen at The Rainbow Gathering in Wyoming.

I customarily keep my tent on the outskirts of the crowd. I like to be on the edge, at the shore of any environment. Anyway, part of my routine, once I'd found my morning walk and song, I'd walk back down to Front Gate and offer my services as a "kooli," helping people haul their stuff into the Gathering. It was a great way to meet people and replenish my weed supply. On one of those excursions, I met a contingent of Hebrew-Jewish-Israelis arriving with their huge supply of Kitchen utensils and food. Loaded up, we made our way into the main Gathering and toward a destination—their scouts had determined—ideal for The Kitchen. They had found the perfect site: an open area, up a hill; "ideal—except for one problem. Some hippy (already) has his tent behind where the Kitchen would be."

Though my middle name is Leavitt (on my father's side), I knew next to nothing about real Jewish people, how they worshipped, never mind what they were doing at an American Rainbow Gathering. I'd heard how the older Jews consider it a "second holocaust"—the way their children are rapidly fleeing from family and tradition. As it turns out, those runaways have found their way to The Rainbow Gathering! Talk about wandering Jews! Many of them followed The Grateful Dead, and the migration trails that bring them back to the Rainbow Gathering every year. Truly wandering, lost Jews. The first that is last, Hu knows. The end... or the beginning? And at any rate...

As we approached the area where my tent was, I sensed that I was about to get an inside view on the Jewish experience. They put down the stuff, and their first task was to establish clear boundaries for the Kitchen area. They measured the area out with something like 600 feet of string. It turned out, wouldn't you know it, that my tent was right behind their main Kitchen tent area, and they wondered if I would be so kind as to move. But I reminded them of where they were, The Rainbow Gathering, and that I would not move my tent for such a reason.

And furthermore, I felt suddenly determined to share in a close encounter with the inner workings of a Jewish spiritual community. They relented—and accepted me. Pretty soon the Rabbis—straight from Israel—arrived with their big fur hats and holy garb. They said prayers all day long, and offered classes on Kabbalah for members of the community. At night we could hear one of the Rabbis calling out to God from further off in the woods. I chimed in as best I could, and heard his responsive laughter.

But what really surprised me was how strenuously, and often, those Hebrews argued with each other. They seemed fixated on failures of responsibility. It went on from morning to night—nonstop bickering. Why didn't you...? Who's supposed to...? Where were you...?—really pressuring one another to get things done! At times they grew heated, and I wondered if they'd ever come to blows. It never happened. The ordinary hippy kitchens made no consistent display of pattern, other than feigning "peace and love"—until someone broke down. So Jerusalem Kitchen was a great example, to me, of an efficient operation. The food was consistently delicious, an alternative to "rainbow stew," pancakes, potato and onion... Actually, after a while, there's an abundance of really amazingly good food everywhere at The Gathering.

Here's what I'm getting at: if I were conversing with someone, but then the Rabbi spoke up, the person I was just talking with would suddenly shift attention to the Rabbi, our conversation suspended in mid-air. This happened all the time. So I watched and listened, and noticed how profoundly attentive they were toward the Rabbi. White hippies have no appreciation for that kind of relationship, that constant attention to a presence, that respect for tradition. We Whites are on our own; our attention to the physicality of spiritual authority long driven from us. I'm an authority unto myself, as James Baldwin reminds us. We've been bred from birth to find our own way: "Do your own thing."

So it was impressive to me (though I didn't know what to do with it), the way those Muslim brothers paid attention to my needs. When I showed them some of my breathing practices, they were amazed that I didn't know how to say the salat. But they could tell when I got thirsty. They seemed undistracted by other stimulations, showing me a quality of respect that only stimulated my "Imam" delusions. Someday, I'll find Muhammad and Omar, Inshallah.

****

When I got back to Anne's, after my first Gathering, she had begun to think of me as "the one"—the one for her. But I didn't share the same romantic feelings. The more resistant I was, the more demanding she became. I had to get out. Once again, Don came to my rescue. Blackie had passed away, and Don had another job helping people with developmental disabilities (DD). He felt unable to do that kind of work, so he asked for my help. We lived in our own two-bedroom apartment in a complex of apartments where about ten different DD people lived. They were all somewhat independent but needed caregivers to make sure they got their meds, arranged appointments, and helped with activities of daily living (ADL). Anne was furious at me for moving out. But I had a job, and she couldn't actually keep me.

Before I say more about Anne, I must share how helpful HDS was for me in making sense of our human characteristics, especially those characteristics I'd be prone to judge in need of therapy. By Design, she was a forceful existential materialist, and, when triggered emotionally, liable to go overboard in trying to secure control. But I'm not an easy person to control, stubborn individual that I am. I had not submitted to her control, and I had a job and wanted to be independent of her. So...

After a few months, predictably, I ran afoul with my job. During med time, in the evening, I was supposed to bring the "consumers" in, one at a time, and thus carefully administer the meds. Instead, I invited them all into the living room office where we could hang out for a good hour of conversation. After a few months of meeting like this, two problems arose. I was making med errors (because I was not concentrating, exclusively on dolling out the meds, and, because I'm prone to mistakes. It's *verboten* to make a single med error in health-related occupations. I had no defense, and promised to do better.

But the second problem was more serious: my boss thought I was "doing psychotherapy" with the "consumers," based on what he heard from them about "med time." Med time had become a very deep and meaningful time for all of us, I thought. As we hung out together, all ten of them with me in the office, I experienced another kind of miraculous transformation in my perception. I literally lost notice of their disabilities.

Had I been hallucinating their DD characteristics, or had they been wearing a mask? They spoke differently, expressed feelings and thoughts clearly; I stopped seeing and hearing the "disability." Maybe I was just listening differently, but it was remarkable. They shared together in a sadness related to the turn-around in Caregivers—"here today and gone tomorrow." They had all learned, early in life, not to trust in the bonds proclaimed by gushing caregiver-social-workers. There's always a new caregiver, and I was soon to become another one.

Anyway, my boss got wind of the routine. He interpreted our "meetings" as attempts to offer "psychotherapy"—based, apparently, on the "positive feedback" he'd been getting. He didn't like it. "You can't practice psychotherapy here." My journey in psychotherapy, and "practicing psychotherapy," had really brought me to the experience of just being myself with others. I wasn't "doing psychotherapy," I was interacting as myself. Sure, I'm grateful for all the education I've had.

Anne began pressuring me to move back in with her. I had nothing to offer—materially. Yet my spirit was still craving leisure, and now I was again out of a job.

What a dilemma I felt: a lack of romantic feelings for Anne but zero desire or energy to "get another job, any job."

I can't explain the stubbornness. Our relationship felt tense, but I also felt a growing frustration with the world. I was frustrated, that people, though perhaps entertained by me, could not understand me. And I was feeling an absurd and ridiculous sort of rage-tantrum toward the White American Zionist agenda. How stupid is America? How stupid am I? I wanted to get out of the country. Go to Indonesia, some crazy place, or back to Canada. Anything to get away. A sense of hopelessness and apathy crept over me and I felt like giving up. All the drama—just quit these delusions and dangerous adventures! A determined urge to withdraw overwhelmed me.

****

Yes! That was it—become a monk! Of course! I remembered how, ten years earlier, I had been to The Pecos Benedictine Monastery in New Mexico for six weeks. I was training as a Spiritual Director. I'd kept in touch with one of the priests, who'd moved to a parish in Florida. Following up on an old request to visit the Monastery, I called them to see if I could come down. They said yes. I told Anne about my desire to go to the Monastery. She agreed, which amazed me, and drove me down to Pecos. She acted strangely calm and accepting, unlike all the other times I had tried to "get away." As I requested, she dropped me off with only a little backpack, a tent, a sleeping bag, and a wooden pipe that I'd carved while living on the street in Victoria. I had no ID or money. She drove away.

As soon as she left, I felt myself finally in the hands of God. To celebrate the moment, I put down my stuff and walked back into the hills behind the Monastery. I had a puff and sang my song—enjoying the echoes off the hills—and wrote in my journal. I had finally come home to myself, really actually surrendered to God. I'd have the routine I longed for. The silence, the discipline, the ease.

Not an hour had passed before I saw a New Mexico police

officer coming through the bush toward me. I couldn't believe it. He called out, "We were looking for someone earlier this morning..." He wondered if I knew anything about it.

Confused, I told him, "I'm associated with the monastery, and I'll be down for evening prayers—let's meet there." He walked away. After a short time I went down to the chapel, hoping the cop had left. Whoever he wanted—I (I think) was not the guy! So I'm sitting in the chapel, sinking into my memories from ten years before, especially the "inner child" healing ceremony. At that time I was also engaged in the practice of the Spiritual Exercises of St Ignatius. My Spiritual Director, Monty Williams, SJ, was holding me for a year to "the first week" of the practice. Anyway, it was my report of this "inner child" healing experience when Monty proclaimed me graduated from "the first week" of the Exercises of St. Ignatius.

It happened after a full day of lectures on the Jungian-Christian-Contemplative approach to "The Inner Child." We were sitting in the pews listening to *Jesu Joy of Man's Desiring*. I was opening myself to memories of "Teddy." As Jesu Joy swelled and moved me, quite suddenly a power came up from below, a bit angry and earnest, demanding: "Where have you been!"... So I'm deep into this memory, really feeling it, when my reverie is interrupted by the cop—asking me the same dumb question: "Did you see the sheriff earlier today?" I really didn't know what this guy was talking about, and I reminded him that we were in a chapel; could we please go outside to talk? We went out, and the Abbot came along, who I remember—and I was happy to see him. But he appeared sullen and dismissive.

His secretary came with him. She asked me to specify the dates, when I thought I had been there. They claimed there was no record of my ever having been at the monastery. So I recounted to him how I knew him, of Fr. Bob, and others. And then quickly went on to share my motivation for coming to the monastery. I reminded the Abbot of the "desert fathers," how they went out to the desert, done with the world and The Church at war, ready for a complete surrender to God! He interjected, "It's not that kind of place." What does he mean? It's a Monastery!—a place for people, like me, who have nothing left to do with their lives but surrender to God! He reiterated, "No, it is not that kind of place." I told him I had no choice, that I'd set my tent outside beneath Our Lady of Guadalupe.

The cop wanted to see my identification, and of course I told him I didn't have any. "I'm right here if you need to know anything."

The Abbot said, "Wait a minute, I think I know where you can stay." He left to make a phone call. Upon his return, he talked briefly with the police officer—who promptly cuffed me. The Abbot said, "There's a place for you in the Santa Fe psyche ward: you can make your surrender to God there!"

As I was being cuffed, I started to sing the daily chant—but loud—"O lord hear my prayer; O Lord hear my cry, when I call come to me!"

When we arrived at the hospital, I was escorted to a holding cell for observation. For two days they looked down on me, a steady stare of lab coats, poised with clipboards. There was nothing for me to do but ponder my situation, my life. Was I the butt of a joke? Did the gods find this funny? I thought, there's got to be someone watching this, besides the lab coats. Here I'd gone to the monastery surrendering to God, and they'd hauled me off to a psyche ward! That sounded like some kinda joke to me, but then, who was laughing? Was I supposed to find this funny?

You get what you're *looking* for, but it's not what you thought. The whole situation crystallized into a perfect resolution—of so many issues in my life having to do with God and psychology. I'd had treatment for sex addiction, but not for mental problems. Here was a chance to embrace my delusional problems. I'd be among others who were facing all kinds of mental and emotional breakdowns. I had to say yes to that!

I thought, let's do this! Two for one: religion and psychology—subsumed in a single event! How fortunate! Recalling how much I had learned from being homeless—I could easily embrace an honest experience on a psyche ward!

I still wouldn't tell the staff anything about myself or where I came from. They didn't need to know I was a Licensed Professional Counselor. I was just another crazy nobody from nowhere, and I was going to make the most of it. I thought I'd try the psychiatric meds, and the Dr. recommended Haldol. I thought it might help to lighten my mood in the absence of weed. But no. After three days on Haldol, I felt a slow creeping "itch" to get out of my skin; it was a futile hunt for a comfortable position. Relaxation felt just out of reach, like a cramped muscle that wouldn't let go.

For a while I kept thinking that I just needed to find a comfortable position, but then I could never find it. I finally started to study the sensation consciously. Like a ubiquitous discomfort with the sensation of my body—at rest! You're just trying to rest, and you can't. It was a hunt for letting go, slipping from my grasp. Relaxation was like a memory I couldn't find. And I really wanted it back. I told the psychiatrist, "If that's the Haldol, no thank you!" I don't know if coming down from a drug constitutes a high, but the progression of sensation, coming back into my body, was tangible. I could feel my body relaxing, like a dog that's been left alone, shivering in the cold, and finally returned to the warmth and comfort of its owner's home.

****

Eager to meet and interact with the other patients, I quickly realized how we all yearned for connection, for a friend, for someone who would really listen, someone patiently and actually interested. I wondered, as I watched the staff, "Why can't you hang out and listen now and then, or is every single interaction limited to checklists and medications? And where are the massage therapists?" As far as I was concerned, the two most important factors in healing—active listening and good touch—were unavailable on the psyche ward. Based on my past experience, human beings need acknowledgement, and, furthermore, they need celebrations for arrival, and for saying goodbye. We want to feel honored for what we've been through.

I felt sad for patients as I watched them walk away from the ward (after weeks!) without saying goodbye, without a celebration, and without a few words of encouragement from the other patients and staff. I had to do what I could to make the experience more meaningful for me, and, hopefully, for the other patients. Before I left, they did implement my idea of having a welcome group for newcomers and a goodbye party for those who were leaving. I felt righteous about making sure they instituted this practice on the ward. Experience is like a sandwich, and how we begin and end makes all the difference in the meaning we derive from what we've been through.

But after ten days, the chief psychiatrist became suspicious of me and told me that I didn't belong on the psyche ward. I'd heard the same message from my therapist at the Sex Addiction treatment center. He mentioned, at the end of my treatment, and sort of in passing, that my presence on the ward was more an expression of some experiential-artistic-philosophical drive. The shrink on the psyche ward did warn me, "It's too easy to end up—back—in a place like this, and you don't want to get into that habit."

Thinking to press the experience a little further, I asked about something that made sense to me. I suggested to the psychiatrist that I could function as a live-in "therapist," live on the psyche ward during the week, and in a cute little apartment in Santa Fe on the weekends! He thought that was an interesting concept, but no. He insisted that I should call someone who could take me—to wherever you really live. He said, "Go Home." So I called Anne (who assumed I'd been settling into monastic life) and asked if she could pick me up at the Santa Fe Hospital. It was the day of the Columbine massacre in Littleton, CO. I remember where I sat in the patient lounge while I watched the TV; the images, the line of kids leaving the school building. I was in a psyche ward.

****

Though I still felt unable to surrender romantically to Anne, I was awed by her determination to have me in her life. When we returned home, she got down on her knees and held my feet, weeping and looking up into my eyes: "You are the one. You are the one." It was abysmal and heartbreaking; I couldn't respond in kind. Still, we were friends... and we were lovers.

David Turnland, one of our friends, had the best parties in Boulder. His huge back yard was a forest of trees; he had a tepee and a wooden shack that was built down into the ground. He taught Western Philosophy at Naropa. A steady stream of spiritual teachers came through his place. Ram Dass came with his weed, traveling Buddhist monks in their amber robes, the Hindu gurus in orange. At one of his parties, I connected with a Hindu Guru named Shangi, a social engineer and a conversational genius. Everywhere he went he would manipulate the conversation with his psychological/spiritual intentions. I was really impressed, not that he was a guru, but as a human being.

We were attracted to each other in some deep way, and in the course of the evening, he convinced me to accompany him back to his ashram in Pennsylvania. He told me I wouldn't have to worry about anything, all my needs would be met. I thought Shangi was a Godsend! I could leave Anne, without being homeless, and continue to enjoy some leisure to pursue my inner interests. When Anne heard about this, she became unglued. David, Shangi and I, and a number of other concerned guests, stuck around long into the night and early morning, trying to deal with Anne's rage about me running off with Shangi. She got so angry and threatening, we called the police so I could have safe passage to Longmont, pack a few things and return to leave with Shangi in the morning.

When I returned to David's house later that night, I resumed my interaction with Shangi, who was still busy guiding a couple of women into some deeper exploration of consciousness. As I approached, he informed me that he was now my "guru" and that I must leave, to another area, and await further instructions.

Stunned, I told him, "I am not looking for a guru; I relate to you as a friend."

We started to argue; he, that he's my guru—now that I have surrendered—and I, on the other hand, that no such arrangement is possible with me. I had no interest in "having a guru." David, who overheard the argument, promptly grabbed my bags, tossed them out the door, and ordered me to leave. Now I really had nowhere to go. But wait. Don to the rescue—again! I pled with David to let me make a phone call. Don answered the phone in a state of such heavy sleep it took him a while to adjust to my reality. But he's a friend—and we both like to say "No Choice."

I couldn't stay at Don's for long, since I didn't work there anymore. However... Anne would still take me back. She'd been telling me, "Love has its own agenda." I don't know why she kept taking me back. Anne is a materialist, with a nice house, two cats, a garden, and a job as a bookkeeper. The truth is, her job as a bookkeeper was torture. I was sure that subjecting herself to a boss was killing her. By design she needed to be her own boss. She came home, every day, furious over some situation at work. We both knew she'd have to strike out on her own, and form her own bookkeeping/accounting practice. So she had left her job and was building her own successful business when I moved back in with her. We both noticed what a difference it made for her: not nearly so angry, and less stress to take out on me.

****

On September 11, 2001, I was sleeping in, as usual, when Anne woke me up and said, "Come see, the world is coming to an end." I made it to the TV just in time to watch the second tower get hit and implode.

It was later in the day—I could see myself, as though I was watching a character in a movie—standing behind a wooden chair in the dining room, my hands on the back of the chair, looking aimlessly around the room. This would be a good time for an epiphany, a vision of direction, or at least a "Next Step."

What I hated was in my face. I had developed a distinct shame toward a caricature, that I could verify in my own experience: this "boss of ya'll American dumb-ass" attitude. The image had grown into an unrelentingly negative character, finally mutating into "the lawless man." I had to identify with that—scary. I couldn't turn away. I am the lawless man. I was ensconced in a System guided by the repulsive image of a man on a cross (minus the understanding of memetic violence), a barcode military regime, raining fire from the skies, disrupting local life all over the Earth—Bible in hand, in the name of Jesus!: "We come to kick your ass and take your shit." That's how a three-time Iraq veteran "explained" it to me.

I suddenly felt called to my own "Mission Accomplished." A very distinct voice in my head said: "Ted, the one surrender you have never made is to America, White America. You are an American, and a WASP American Zionist—to boot. Stop resisting! Accept your role. Accept your people. You are in the theater now. Start your new life from here. Say Yes to America!"... I thought, omg... that's true! I have never accepted this aspect of my story. I would have to stop running from "the American dumb ass" (in me!) and say Yes to the American that I am—whatever that means!

...And seal it by saying Yes to Anne! The voice went on. "OK, you're on the Cross of Migration, Ted, so only commit for seven years (at a time). Seven years is a whole lifetime. Commit to Anne for seven years. She really loves you... and you really love her, after all—you're here!" Like it or not, we wake up with the people we love. You can "love the one you're with." I did surrender to her love, and felt it as a mutual thing. Love does have its own agenda. I still had my one condition: no pressure to "get a job!" I needed more time to verify the linguistics of The HDS. She accepted my bargain. We planned a great ceremony, and proclaimed ourselves married. We put up a big tent in the backyard, invited all our Dance Home friends, Anne's whacky Denver family, and had a huge party. We announced to everyone, shamelessly, that we were making a seven-year commitment, and as an extension of our relationship, we would "build community." Which meant having a lot of dance parties. I think it was the happiest day of my life.

****

When I moved back in with Anne, one of the ways she encouraged me was to pay for me to take an American Sign Language class at CU. I was so grateful for that, and thought it would definitely be useful in developing my public abstract dance/sign practice on Pearl St. But I had a strange experience instead. About halfway through the semester, I looked around the room and realized I was back in grade school. Of the fifteen people in the class, I estimated myself to be where I had always been: almost at the bottom, maybe a DD person and a thickheaded jock up from the lowest rung. Confronted with a sense of choice, I thought: either I would have to ask the teacher to focus her teaching on me, the slow guy... or quit. In a fit a solidarity with my grade school self, I cut my losses and disappeared during a class break. What a wicked feeling of delight: walking away from that classroom as though I'd finally rescued my ten-year-old self from his misery: "Come on, let's get outta here!"

The (Re)Gathering Dogma

It was with great relief that the ordinary conflict between Anne subsided after the "marriage" ceremony. Having quit her job, she quickly became self-employed and experienced a peace of mind she hadn't known before. Commitment provided me with a protective space for exploring the strange mutation churning through me.

The teenager (the "Biblical Time" of life) in me, the character I called "Waheybi," had only begun his taming: "Wait for your inner Response to others, then take your time and notice what you're feeling—never speak or act spontaneously." The development of patience requires time—for the solar plexus—to process the emotional wave. And for me, passing sensitive feelings through a registry of composites before making any important decision. It was as though Waheybi had first to blast through the past, and express himself—defying the suffocating layers of shame and blame and guilt—and discover again where the boundaries among human beings really are. At some point, the sense of punishment (healthy shame and guilt) educated him to verify when he was not following his own strategy and authority. It became obvious, when he provoked a negative reaction, that he had initiated where he had no business. Who asked you? No one to blame—not even himself. Generators make the greatest fools, leaping off roofs as though Manifestors.

Our commitment also gave us a chance to negotiate Ann's jealousy, and my loyalty, with less mind-bending drama. Dance Home provided the opportunity, every Tuesday and Friday night. We could dance with other partners and talk about our feelings. I have two ways of dancing: spinning like a top by myself, in contact improv with random partners, or sign-dancing like an idiot. Anne and I often danced together, or we danced with others, or a whole group of others, tumbling around in a mass of bodies, or weaving around each other. It's a wonderful sensation: to close your eyes and feel "The Body"—a delight that transcends preoccupation with the sexual binary. Every body is of The Body.

The challenge, for Anne and me, was the female newcomer—were she to "accidentally" initiate a dance with me, Anne would interrupt, throwing in an angry accusation, usually on the assumption that the new woman and I indeed secretly knew each other—and were about to elope! Her outbursts were so outrageous, to me, that I could avoid my worst flaw: getting serious! And besides, I was really happy in my life with her, and no longer had any desire to escape. I was getting what I wanted, after all.

Now I had a chance to experience the polar side of my original marriage to Lesley who had every reason to be jealous but never projected that energy, nor indulged in my lustful interests. So it was a strange kind of delight: to meet Anne's jealousy with the feeling that it could be a healing experience for both of us. It was also a chance for me to validate The Human Design System, as her behavior did not require any deeper analysis than what I saw in her chart, and from our experience together. A good explanation can overcome the blame-virus. When you see the integrity, of both self and not-self, you are deprived of any negative judgement. We may still judge and find error, but we can no longer blame the self and the not-self. People have more integrity than I thought. It's our minds that are fucked up. Here she is, an existential ego, a manifesting materialist, her sense of control threatened, losing focus, and going overboard—an angry Manifestor. That's what to expect. Acceptance is the therapy. HDS was giving me a chance to behave therapeutically without pretending to be a therapist.

****

My relationship with Anne provided leisure for exploring my evolving interests in the world. I hadn't read a single book in three years, and thought I might never read again, happy just to memorize the Rave I Ching. But one day I surprised myself, as I walked by a garage sale and noticed a book that has always terrified me (and still does): "The Critique of Pure Reason," by Kant. I started to read. While I still didn't understand a thing, it dawned on me that I could study the world again through the linguistic lens of the Human Design System! I never did get far with Kant; but I appreciate his use of ten categories for chunking concepts, and his intriguing assumption that we invent "space and time"—in order to think about all the other things, the stuff that's "there/real." At any rate, the thought of HD as a linguistic lens, useful for integrating information, lit a fuse that burned through the next seven year ("life cycle") with Anne. I entered a monastic-research cave, time to review all the subjects I'd ignored or rejected due to my previous ("aspect") fixation on theology and psychology.

I found the capacity of the HDS to synthesize and integrate the information I was reading fascinating. Proceeding like Kant, I organized my reading in terms of the ten Stages (categories) of the Prenatal Sequence according to HDS. I was working on the theory that if HDS is what Ra says it is, then I should be able to verify any thoughtful research, science-oriented or not, and that it should illuminate some aspects of the categories and show their relative place in The Sequence. Protagoras said (something like), "Man is the measure of all things." The HDS claims to be a formula for proving the uniqueness of Homo sapiens: the one who times and measures the world (unknowingly), even as he walks around, busy or bored.

Obsessed with this theory, I went to the Longmont Public Library once a week. Starting in the "New Books" section, I sought for titles on History/evolution/Judaism... Cosmology/ gnosticism... Geometry/Hinduism... Philosophy/Western... Chemistry/Islam/The Tribe... general Science/Native spiritualities... physics/Chinese wisdom... political economy/the breath... biology/Christianity... and Math/Buddhism. I was not seeking an in-depth understanding of each area, but enough to articulate a relation between the book I was reading and one of the ten dimensions on the Prenatal Sequence, and the Nine Centers on the human Body Graf.

I had already summarized my obsession with antiquated and unsatisfying religious problems in a tome I titled "The Gathering Dogma." It was the writing-rant of a pissed-off thirteen-year-old. My attempt was to understand the nature of Religion through the centers of the body—as exemplified by human evolution, etc. My personal obsession was to see All the religions of the world through The Body Graf! So here's a partial (limited to the Religious Aspects) summary of my research. (See Appendix #1.)

****

I so appreciate the gift of leisure (the basis of culture) that allowed me to be absorbed in Research. Most of my time is spent on research. I appreciate all the books that opened the world to me in a new way. I seem to carry some fundamental religious conservative with me—turning reading itself into a kind of (liberal?) religion. The more I read, the more I wondered if the human problem centers on simple ignorance about the world. Are we not here to understand our conscious relationship to the world?—not to grasp some final cause, but to remain open to learning? Are we not an expression of the capacity for endless learning?—to keep learning, never certain in our conclusions? I now sense again a measure of my own religious intolerance, this time toward people who just don't read enough! or who don't read beyond a narrow range of interest.

If you are not reading, how can you develop an appreciation for all the different ways of being human? We seem in a rush to crystallize our thinking, and then avoid, violently, the call to "think again!" (the meaning of repentance, and Philosophy per se, I remind you!). We seem to hate to have our minds changed about anything. I still do. If I hear something that challenges me, my first impulse is to fling myself into verbal combat. My only progress, and consolation to others, is to encourage them to relax at the physical level. No harm! As long as we're afraid of each other, our differences, too easily, lead to physical violence. Thus, we will never have the deep conversations we need to have.

I had leapt into a kind of Liberal abyss. My vast reading led me to see how the different religions of the world are distortions around the proper functioning of the human form, as though the outer conflicts between religions occur inside every human body—to ensure "perpetual war." Human Religion tends to fixate on an aspect of human nature, and fails to comprehend The Whole. Any single religion is but a reflection of one of ten dimensions of The Body. No single religion has the whole picture. No religion is special (unless it's Islam)—compared to the others. No wonder we get sick. As long as we don't see The Whole, we must take the view of aspects. This is the core of our human linguistic problem: We love our aspects. This keeps the program running. But now we do have a vision of The Whole, and It's a She! And She... is a beautiful... Conception!

****

My Dad represented Christianity for me, and when he died, so did my (practicing) bond to Christianity. My brother came up from San Antonio, and we drove up to Calgary together for Dad's funeral. Dad had been suffering from some heart trouble. When the doctors opened him up they, apparently, nicked his spleen, and he died. I didn't quite understand how to think of that—he died by accident. It was his time to go. My brother and I were in a new place—in relationship to the beliefs we were raised with. [Though, it seems, he has returned to "hellfire and brimstone" at the end.] At the funeral service, we were given a chance to share our reflections on Dad's life.

When it came my turn, I said, to the completely evangelical audience, that Dad had demonstrated "the way of the friend" to me. It was not his evangelism that I remembered, it was his friendliness toward everyone he saw and met. He was as friendly to beggars as he was to Brahmins. It always embarrassed me, as a kid, how easily he could walk up to strangers and have conversations. Sure, we knew he had his agenda: to steer every conversation to "Jesus" as soon as he could. What matters to me now was that he showed me, practically, that to follow Jesus is *the way of The Friend*—or Christianity doesn't mean a thing! And when Dad died, I also felt as though the form of Christianity, that he represented, died with him. I don't see the Christian world today as friendly—not at all. If the Christian world, the very world that dominates the world today through our WASP American Zionist political form, remembered "what a friend we have in Jesus," they would rise up overnight and end the lawlessness that is America today.

I still wasn't through processing all my feelings about Dad. It would take a few more years for me to recognize how amazing his story is; and how significant his story is for understanding the deeper issues of my White culture. What is forgiveness, really? My Dad's story tells it all. It's the story of the patriarchy—at its end. My Dad is my messiah. I say it now with tears of gratitude.

****

My relationship with Anne came to a glorious end when a bunch of obsessed poets seduced me to join their Symposium on a tour of the West Coast. An aspiring movie maker, Rob and his friend Rob, were making a movie about poetry in America. It was filmed as an escape from New York City, and focused on a few Boulder poets who would form the core of the movie. The poets had invited me to participate in their Symposiums. These were gatherings that consisted of poetry readings accompanied by voice improv, drums, guitars, a keyboard, and Bruce, a professional oboist. I contributed with "industrial acoustics" and interpretive whirling, expressing the spirit of the poetry and music through movement. What an ecstatic experience! Though I did not consider myself a poet, the Symposium brought fresh meaning to my life. And for some reason, they encouraged me to (try to) write poetry.

****

Troy, my master poet and writing coach, was to play a central role in the movie. I had just finished writing "The Gathering Dogma." Troy forced himself to read a few pages of my tome, and flatly declared that I was really a poet and must learn the form as quickly as possible. I don't know what his intuition was, but he couldn't read my pedantic pricks. His first instruction was to consider smashing my precious tome to pieces— and begin writing again, by writing poetry. But I had no concept of myself as a poet.

Troy did manage to interest me in his writing practice. I'd had a basic aversion to reading poetry, and even after meeting Troy, I didn't read books of poetry for another three years. Poetry had never attracted me, not for as long as I could remember. I had two reasons. It was incomprehensible, and even when you thought about what it might mean, so what, it could still mean anything. Why be interested in obscura? Who has time to figure out what a poem means? And then, my (immediate) boredom with (obvious) rhyme. I mean, pick up a thick volume of 18th Century poetry at any page, and you'll find the same thing... da da da da da doo da da da da da boo. Endlessly... on and on, page after page. That was my basic sense of poetry; and I didn't care to put on airs, or slave over rhymes.

I remember the first poem I ever wrote—the first "write a poem" assignment in school. I think it was a grade eight English class. My first blush with poetry, the terror of the command: "Write a poem!" All I could do was follow my pencil down to the page... I'm in a room... and... desolate room after desolate room after desolate room, with no way out but a door to yet another desolate room. There was no escape. I couldn't get out of the poem, nor could I fake my way out. It was completely depressing, and discouraged me from ever writing, never mind reading, poetry again. They published my poem it in the school paper.

But under Troy's tutelage, I tried to accept his faith in my—obviously hidden talent—and started to write a poem a day. I'm still a religious guy. When I find something interesting, and surrender to it, the power of routine carries into practice. Anyway, three years later, I started reading poetry. And I fell in love, discovering a true friend, more, a lover in the distance, closer, like my jugular.

****

Such thoughts would make you think I had walked away from Anne so easily. Her running into an old boyfriend, while I was on the Pink Elephant tour, was an ironic godsend. I had no confidence, during our relationship, that after seven years she would let me go—with grace. We could not have planned a better completion experience... and a chance to revisit my old friend, lust. I had become so content with myself, and my life situation; I thought maybe lust was a thing of the past. I did not fully appreciate the feeling of contentment, of libidinal calm, until those nights, after I returned, when Anne would spend the evening with her boyfriend. Lust is a colossal waste of time and energy! Thinking about what she must be doing with him... right now!... are her legs... does she hold his head... ah... awful fantasies, vivid, churning energy.

I had grown to enjoy the calm pleasure of reading—without any distraction! Now I found Lust again, quivering over the page, translucent energy patterns, banishing the letters and any rational thought—to the slime pit of lustful jealousy. All I could do was hang out with it. What came to me was that lust and jealousy are two sides of the same bloody coin. You can imagine your partner with someone, and feel lust, or you can feel jealous; but in either case you've concocted a fantasy about what they might be doing! At any rate, I was happy for Anne. They did have a more supportive connection, even by Design. They were both oriented by practicality and the mundane, happy to spend the day fixing the house and watching a movie at night.

****

On my birthday in 2008, I arranged a move back to Boulder. My poet friend Mark, with his wife and two sons, invited me to stay on their porch for as long as I needed. I had to remember how I'd survived previous, crushing, experiences of missing a partner after a breakup. It always feels like the first time, or the worst time... always more painful than ever. Experience might have told me I would survive, but the wound still hurt like hell, like the hurt would remain forever. Letting go can feel impossible. I felt so heartbroken, walking down the sidewalks, crying as though the pavement would cave in with grief.

I can miss someone for at least three months, every day, for significant hours of the day, relentless yearnings to reconnect, struggling and resisting the requirement of letting go. How do you let go? I can't. I have to be patient and take my time. And during those months, no one else could get in; not really. I thought maybe I would jump right in with someone else, but the feeling of hypocrisy was too intense, and whoever the "transitional object" might be would know I wasn't present. And besides, I've come to appreciate how connected Jonny is to my emotional system. If I don't feel committed, he is not going to stand up! Grief is no turn-on. I'd had the same kind of feelings for Lesley, who I missed consciously, for three years.

I was finally ready to get back on my feet. Waheybi was somewhat tamed. It felt vulnerable to be active in the world again after at least ten years of not working. I did have a referral to a senior care company called "Dignity Care." It was the most obvious thing for me to do, if not a place to start in my process of "getting back into the world." It was not many days working as a caregiver, however, that I realized how appropriate "senior care" was in the trajectory of my exploration of the WASP American Zionist—in me. What better way to find out than accompany them through "end of life care:" from the time when they can still walk and talk, to lying down, to becoming dumb, stop eating... and drinking, the transition of active dying, to observe the "fish-lip-kiss" of the final breath, and the unbelievable stillness after. I listened to their stories, and they loved mine! I had finally found my most appropriate audience and my true calling: end-of-life care... in White America.

And then, (I want to say, of course, lover that I am) my next seven-year life cycle began in a dance with Joy. Joy, the messenger of miracles.

O Happy Dream

I returned to Boulder on my birthday (in honor of my inner ten-year-old): a dramatic gesture of "sink or swim." I'd end up homeless again, or I'd get a job. My license to practice psychotherapy was a thing of the past. I felt like a freshman, or fresh out of high school with nothing much to show for myself. So, the day after moving onto Mark's front porch I went to a place called Dignity Care and applied for a job. The woman who interviewed me assured me that I was just the kind of person they were looking for: a retired psychotherapist with a rich and varied life experience, someone comfortable with death. I didn't let on how "varied" my life experience really (still) was. There was something appropriate, I sensed, about working with old white people; having already worked with children, teenagers, families, as well as adult individuals and group therapy. So, "End of Life Care" was in the flow of things.

I soon reached the conclusion that the current state of White American decay may be told through Nursing Home eyes, and I was properly initiated on my first day of work. It was unbelievable. Perhaps I was impressionable, and naive about the reality of "senior care," but what I experienced that day was a shock for me. It was as though the gods had, once again, arranged the whole scenario just for me. The assignment was meant to provide an easy way for me to break into the job: "just go to that Nursing Home and have lunch with a lady who has Alzheimer's." We were to eat in a side room, and then go for a walk around the complex.

Arriving early, I thought I'd first walk around the facility and get a feel for the place. Walking around the halls, I had the feeling of entering a twilight zone, or one of Dante's rings around the borders of hell. A plaintive and desperate voice called from a room with the door ajar, "Henry, are you there? O Where are you Henry?" Along the main hallway, and in front of the nursing station, sat a row of old bodies slumped over in wheelchairs. One of the old women was trying repeatedly and unsuccessfully to get her foot up on to the foot-rest. Just that simple thing. Her eyes, full of anguished request, were darting from her foot to the environment. I could see how desperate her little struggle was, and that she'd never get her foot on the foot-rest.

I walked on—I'm not a good Samaritan on my first day of work. I wanted to be like a fly on the wall, bearing no responsibility, but to observe: How have things always happened here? The only black woman I've ever seen in a Boulder Nursing Home had parked her wheelchair at a crossing where four hallways meet. Her voice was loud and commanding, like she was at Church, "O my king and my God... do not rebuke me in your anger or discipline me in your wrath... have mercy on me for I am faint." Anyone quoting the Bible gets my attention. I can't believe what I'm hearing.

Walking further down another hall, I encountered a woman wearing only a nightshirt. It seemed as though her face had been deliberately scratched, and I really hated to think of it, but she looked just like a zombie. She actually lumbered toward me, arms reaching forward, pleading: "Have you been sent to deliver us?"

I think, "What?!" Is this staged? I turned and walked away, like that's the last straw—I'm being set up! Am I really on a secret mission, to find the real end of the American Dream: this Nursing Home?! Here it is, Welcome... what?! I felt mystically perplexed, the awful reinforcement of my very delusions! Who sent me on this mission? I'm Not a Believer! Because I know I don't know God. Is this really happening? What's going on here? And then, to top my initiation off, another old woman points at me, and continues pointing as she walks over to me, takes my right hand and begins caressing it firmly, lifting it very slowly towards her face.

Before anything serious happened, a couple of nurses rushed over and rescued me from her, informing me, with certainty, "She'll be all over you if I let her go on." I'd been on psyche wards, lock-up facilities, and jails, but that first day at the Nursing Home was the weirdest social experience in my life.

When it was time for me to see Betty, I went to the Alzheimer's unit. A nurse introduced us. Betty was sitting at a table with a few of the other residents. I pulled up a chair around a cozy table, and we all crowded around. It was my first time socializing with an entire group of people with Alzheimer's. Perhaps because I knew what it was like to be high—I fit right in: Stay present-centered, no past or future reference, let the world unfold—it can seem funny, if not strange. When you know you don't know, doesn't mean somebody does. They had an inclination to laugh about everything; that they, and now we, were members of a secret society of those who "got the big joke." It really felt that way: everything was funny, and absurd. Or just more proof for Laughter Yoga.

As my visits with Betty stretched into weeks, I began to notice how happy she'd become to see me. She would dress a little better and wear some makeup. Then I learned that, in her mind, I'd been transformed from an ordinary caregiver into an old lover, or husband. I was no longer me. Betty was simply carrying on a relationship with someone who'd left, and had now returned—to her great joy! Yet she never said anything to me about it but may have assumed that I knew perfectly well what was going on. When her daughter (who hired me) caught on, that was the end of it, and my first failure as a caregiver. I'd have to imagine what the daughter feared; I never found out. There's a lost conversation.

****

My challenges as a caregiver are more interesting than my successes. There are times, in the presence of someone with dementia, that can feel impossible. Dementia seems to become apparent in the year or two before actively dying: at the interface of physical breakdown and some internal illusion of still being in control. (That's my analysis.) So that remembered state returns, in the present, as a trance—of complete competence. In such a state, they rule the roost. They know exactly what's going on, what needs to get done, and when! They do not question their reality. I was a participant in an experience of their past.

One woman I lived with (as a live-in caregiver) had been a beautiful and competent host for family events and gatherings. Such a trance would come over her late in the evening, but that didn't matter. She knew my job was to take her shopping and not to ask questions.

Now get the car out front! She went on about provisions and various preparations for the onslaught of family members descending on the house first thing in the morning. Getting up on her walker, she would stomp toward the front door and order me again to get the car... But it's after 11... No, it's not, we have plenty of time... I'm not comfortable going out with you this late at night, and I haven't heard about anyone coming tomorrow. Besides, it's time now to get ready for bed... No, it's time for shopping, Ted! Your job is to help me. You have been so helpful up to now, and you are really starting to disappoint me!... But we just can't go out now, it's too late... You bastard!... Then she would charge at me with her walker, trying to force her way by me and out the door. Those were moments when I tried to be as therapeutic as I knew how. I would try to point out the facts. Then I would discuss the possibility of parallel worlds. In the next round I would praise her for her capacity for hospitality, and how competent she was as a mother and entertainer of guests... I'd concede, "I can totally understand how incompetent I must be, given how you see the situation now."... Then I would talk about the fact that children have their own set of problems, and adults have their own set of problems, and seniors also have their own set of problems... and you are having one of those senior problems right now!

I didn't mind applying labels—verboten in senior care: "Never tell a senior they have dementia." But I think using the definition at certain times can ease the understanding. It's natural for old people to experience "dementia." Or something. It happens. I personally think dementia is a last-ditch attempt by old people to get some therapy for unresolved emotional fixations... Maybe they want to know: "Who can meet me in this painful, unfinished place? What is there to lose? It's time to go crazy!

I was interested in the experience as a kind of validation for the nature of human therapy, based on the general human need for healing. Why not be with them in it and expose my own limitations? Why lie? Why pretend? Finally, sitting back down, with me next to her, something would finally shift. She would say... "Well, maybe everything is going to be alright after all. "Yes! That's it! I really think so too. Now I'm tired, let me help you get to your bed...

Then she'd wake up again, two hours later, and I'd hear her, through the baby monitor, trying to get out of bed. I'd force myself up to find out what the rustling sounds were all about. She'd had a dream. Well, she'd just returned from a real event. It was a great party. The decorations were beautiful, and (of all things!) I had given a wonderful speech!—which had been recorded, and she had it all on a video tape! And I should help her look for it!... It's around here somewhere. Old people just need to know that someone cares...when it's messy.

****

Another old lady I lived with had a great old house on "The Hill" in Boulder. It had the feel of a big cabin. It was located west of CU campus, heading up into the first rise of the Rockies. She had raised her kids there, and "back in the day," it was the only house around. There used to be a husband, but he disappeared one day and left her with the children. It was a painful story; she didn't care to talk about it. But she had managed; worked hard and invested well; and raised four children, all successful.

She had a great library of books, and was proud of them. Her attitude was secular and scientific, doubting everything— but with a playful side that wanted to be teased with probability. I came to think of her as an icon of the American dream; actually, the fulfillment of Christianity—according to the Canadian philosopher Charles Taylor. People with a secular conscience are today's most evolved "Christians." A secular conscience does not need dogma. Belief is not a requirement for having a sense of conscience. They don't need to use "God" to make sense of anything or everything, nor do they need to understand why they conclude as they do. It's OK not to know, and they don't care that they don't know. But they can philosophize any time, and enjoy that conversation— above anything!

Only the dying can really feel free to think openly. Here was a white woman, someone who really lived a perfected secular conscience, unafraid to die, self-accepting and in no need of grand explanations.

Now, I don't care what my American bosses say; behind

closed doors, I tell seniors that I am a member of their Extended Family. Someone from the scattered homo sapiens tribe return-ing to care for grandmother/grandfather when no one else can. Would you invite a stranger off the street to wipe your bottom? I have walked into homes where perfectly capable adults sit around, but they need a caregiver to help grandpa get into the shower, make sure his bottom gets cleaned, get him out of the shower, dried and dressed... and then I leave—never to see them again! We think that's the normal human thing to do.

Pericare is such an important part of senior care. I almost convinced—the last senior I cared for—that friends had plans to make a movie of our bathroom routine, so they needed us to practice and choreograph the whole routine. We laughed so hard, suspended in the air, somewhere between the wheel-chair and the toilet. Would we do it for comedy or science? The kind of conversations you can have, getting from the wheelchair to the toilet and back, are some of the deepest con-versations I've had in my life. What is this life all about? Does life still have meaning when you're in the midst of a transfer? In the act of being transferred. May Philosophy enlighten the transference, "making" room for Grace.

You might say that caregiving isn't rocket science. I'd argue with you. Getting someone from a wheelchair to a toilet requires preparation and measurement. It's easy to hurt your back—trying to hold someone up, when they start to fall, and you're not in a good position. Old people and their caregivers all have stories about falling, and falling together. And when the knees give way, you know the end is nigh.

It took me a while to feel my body engage with caregiv-ing routines. Any routine requires time for learning—how to bring the mind's attention (from wherever the hell it is) to the body—which is always now. We make a habit of negotiating interpersonal space with our hands and arms, thus express-ing the mind. But the mind (like fingers to elbow) can't hold anything up without support from your own hips, feet and knees. I hurt my back and had to wear a brace for a year, until I took the mechanics seriously, and applied what I knew from contact improv dance to the transfers. You get close, and comfortable, with weight-bearing hugs.

I'll try to describe an ordinary caregiving routine. When it was time for bed, I wheeled Patricia to the toilet. Reaching for a handle, for example, her arms would ease through the air in the slow reach of an orangutan, with focus and grace. Her shoulder joints and arm muscles were sore, toughened by the struggle of holding herself up in the chair all day. She refused to use the recliner, which I had encouraged her son to bring over. No, she had to sit bolt upright all day in that wheelchair as though it was her solemn duty.

It used to bug me, watching her struggle with discomfort. I felt like a witness to an ongoing penance. When she became tired and sleepy, she really had to press down with her elbows in order to stay upright. Most old people in America hold on to their stubborn individuality; that's OK, but the refusal of comfort seems like a disease that affects the elderly. It took me a while to celebrate it, weirdly, as a last expression of independence, of valiant and worthy work. The recliner... too lazy.

Old people (especially white people) really need comfort, especially physical touch and interesting conversation. One old lady I worked with refused to lie down on the couch, so she sat there, for months before she died, with her head between her knees. It was a sign of laziness for her to lie down on the couch. A couple of times I convinced her to try, but after a few minutes, her conscience would get the better of her, and she'd sit up again. So I'd prop her up with pillows on both sides, and sometimes a couple of pillows on her lap in front of her so at least she wouldn't fall through her knees to the floor.

So then we'd sway for a while so her feet got a feeling for movement, just an inch and then another, nice and safe, until the wheelchair was right behind her knees. With one arm still around her lower waist, I would reach down to the arm of the wheelchair to support my own back and ease her down into the chair... I want to see that movie, and all the great conversations along the way. The gods were there... someone had to be watching.

****

A man I worked with recently seemed to be heading into active death. He was in the Navy during WWII, and we had long conversations about that war, and other wars. We listened to a book on tape, called "Inferno," and agreed that if more people read the book, they could be dissuaded from repeating such horror, which happened in those years in every corner of the globe.

His PhD was based on an obscure Spanish play, in which he tried to prove that another scholar had made a translation error in her own famous treatise. We discussed Don Quixote, the Ottoman Empire, Lincoln's life, and the Civil War; we wondered what really happened under Reconstruction. Why were there no black soldiers at the centenary celebrations? Did the North really bring equality to African Americans?

We shared our poems. In the last three days that I was with him, he began hallucinating, all day long, certain that things were going on that I could not see: that I was someone else or that we could go out and "get some chilly," which he never ate.

He often thought his wife was there. At one point, he struggled to sit up, reaching forward as though a child were rushing into his arms. He said it was "a four-year-old."

At times, I reviewed for him his condition, as a supposedly dying man, that his mental boundaries in space and time were falling apart... and everything was normal, but that, "Right now we really can't get your shoes on or go outside."

I would remind him that his body could hardly stand and

wouldn't without a lot of close support. He laughed about that and agreed, but in the next moment, he would be emphatic again, "We must get going."

It was eleven at night, and there was nowhere to go and nothing to do. But he was in momentum, and I had no choice. I labored with him as we strove to get him out of bed and standing up with his walker. I trusted that the exhaustion he felt would bring his mind naturally to his limitations. I would put my gait belt around his waist since he still wanted to walk to where he was going. I felt that I was witnessing one of those critical/mystical moments in life: do you remember the last time you walked?

We'd make it to the living room, where he would see his familiar old recliner across the room. He would stumble quickly across the room, where I'd help him collapse heavily into his chair. He'd lean back, exhausted, as though he'd climbed a steep mountain slope. I'd read some of his own poems aloud. After only a few minutes, he'd suddenly snap the recliner up, his arms reaching forward into thin air, his eyes wide and open, ablaze with delight, exclaiming, "Well!"... because the four-year-old was back and springing into his arms.

He lives in assisted living housing. It's a pretty nice place, and the seniors seem to enjoy hanging out with each other. Some of them are still couples, most are single. I never saw or heard noisy children in the place. But it's not a place to die. In America, a lot of old people leave their homes to live in assisted living units, and from there to a nursing home or hospital, where they finally do die.

****

When I feel connected with seniors, we naturally share thoughts and feelings about aging, and aging in America. I can get worked up about the way I see and experience the American attitude toward their elders. It's hard for me not to see the signs of decay, the decay of Empire; the end of The Dream.

Is there not a loss of meaning for a culture whose old and young are so fundamentally separated? I wonder. Children in this corner, teenagers over there, adults minding their own business, and seniors locked away in "homes." How can the stories be passed on, when there are no children around to hear them? What does the "greatest generation" mean when there are no children to understand what's "great" about it? Can greatness be transmitted by a news reporter or a book? Is greatness the memory of all the people we've had to kill to stay "great"?

I had just been reading "Remnants of Auschwitz, The Witness and the Archive," by Giorgio Agamben, and was startled to see a relationship (in my mind) between the utter loss of meaning, not only in the image of the "mussel manners" in the Nazi prison camps, but also in that image of all the old white people lined up in wheelchairs. Is that a meaningful image? I call it meaningless. Furthermore, unless you've spent time in a Nursing Home or had many experiences with people dying in their homes, ordinary Americans have no experience of being present with the dying process, never mind the process of dying where you're surrounded, often, by strangers. Children certainly are not present. Do I not, as a caregiver and witness to this nightmare, have a role to play in this scene of meaninglessness? Look at the endless wheelchairs, lined up against the wall—that's meaningless to me.

I once shared my views with one of the seniors responsible for a social event centered on discussions of relevant ideas, news items, local issues. She invited me to give a talk. The room was packed. It'd been announced that "Mr. Garrison is coming to share his thoughts about the American family." And I did share, as honestly as I could, just these thoughts: that old white people in America are being led through another holocaust, and that they, all the caregivers, might as well be mussel manners! In the big picture of things, is this a meaningful way to die? Or are we the first to be experiencing the death of a culture?

They just looked at me, and most of them nodded, like it's a secret that's being kept from the culture at large. The point is, for me, no one seriously disagreed. They didn't drive me out at the mention of a parallel to the Holocaust. Maybe I'd struck a cord. Maybe I'll be accused of minimizing the Holocaust and making it as special as Jesus. The Holocaust just is our clearest demonstration of human meaninglessness. And I'm saying, you can see the same kind of problem when you see all the wheelchairs—merely suspended in space, no connection to anything humanly meaningful. I suggested to them that, as a witness, my relative responsibility is to make it known. Meanwhile, the young Hebrews are fleeing their nests to follow the Grateful Dead.

****

Due to financial concerns, and because he's actively dying, the latest man I care for is moved to a nursing facility where he (his body) can be watched more carefully. I'm no longer needed but am asked if I would accompany him in the ambulance to the nursing home. He had asked me to stay with him to the end... of his life. I have to break my promise, and feel like a hypocrite. As we climb out of the ambulance, he says, "I just want to know when I can go home." No one says anything. He is as "home" as can be, and he will die surrounded by strangers. When I insist on visiting, my care manager tells me I have to deal with my "dependency issues." I feel angry and suggest to her that I don't have dependency issues, but that America, and us caregivers, have unfelt grief issues, and that caregivers should be the first to acknowledge the death of The American Empire! I suggested the need for a caregiver grief group—to be the first who might acknowledge the decay of this System—this Babylon.

I always felt a little deprived when I missed the death of someone for whom I was a caregiver. But I was there for the death of the woman who had assisted in choreographing our bathroom procedures. And attending her death was a perfectly choreographed routine. Somehow, I knew she was at the portal, and I sensed the sublime. It was after sunset and no one else was around. I picked up my guitar and strummed the tune-up chords for the Welcome Home Song. At the end of the last Buddhist Hrii, I moved to stand at her side and looked down into her face, watching her take her last gentle breath, the "fish lips"—when the lips, in one last attempt to breathe, pucker, but no air passes. A true kiss. And then, I stood transfixed in a stillness beyond belief. I stood there for at least ten minutes. I could not move away from the sense of the sacred. Strange, yet beautiful; death in America, where strangers—like angels (or devils)—are hired to keep bottoms clean and attend the final kiss goodbye.

****

Having written my Gathering Dogma while with Anne, I envisioned the following seven years to be something along a Gnostic theme, having less to do with the grand outer framework of universals and more focused on my own story and inner experience of the same. I even wondered if I might head to Missouri and hook up with the Mormons. Now, I'm hoping, at least, to make a pilgrimage to Adamandamon. [Which I'll do in the next volume, wait and see.]

Dance Home was, I argued, a spiritual practice, not a dance club or a pickup joint. Yet I was bound to meet new women at Dance Home. I had never seen Joy at Dance Home before. Her bubbly presence permeated the space, like a child, giddy, squealing with delight. We did have a short dance, and I let go as usual at the end of the song. I naturally presented myself as an example of detachment, for the sake of our dance practice. For example, when the song ends—there's a gap, so you both let go, move on, new dance. I always interrupted special sub-groups by spinning in the middle of them.

So I resisted the urge to pursue Joy on the dance floor and walked out at the end. I was putting on my shoes and getting ready to leave. As I stood up, Joy burst through the door of the dance hall, staring at me intently. So, like a fool, I asked her calmly, intrigued by her dancing eyes, "What's your story?"

"Do you mean, am I available?"

There was no resistance, and I fell like a puppy into her life. We talked for hours. She spoke of her dedication to A Course In Miracles. Should I groan or be happy? I had read enough of ACIM to see that it fit, for me, and weirdly, as The mystical theme for the Western Philosophical mind! The Savior, lifting our mental oppression from the holding of grievances, memetic violence, war. But I just couldn't surrender to the language. The last thing I wanted to do, again, was talk about Jesus. And the orientation toward "the ego" really bugged me. HDS had left me content with my ego—in the understanding of my own *mechanics*. But then It came to me that ACIM must be in the Gnostic trajectory, and after all!—I was just entering the Gnostic phase in my research!

I always need some overarching-vision-of-meaning before I can surrender the energy of my life to a project. If I can't see the big picture, I'm not interested. But if I can see the big picture, the details then become secondary. And Joy's details were not compatible with mine. Her chart and mine don't have a single electromagnetic connection, which I had thought was really important! "Love has its own agenda," I heard in my ear. Whatever the technicalities were, Joy and I were very drawn to each other... and the attraction grew. I guess love is not about compatibility.

Six months later I moved down to Littleton, to live with Joy, and surrender to the daily practice of ACIM. I had always found reading ACIM like wading through psychic mud. The language irked me. Then one day, in frustration, I did something I had never heard done with ACIM: I read it with passion and zeal, like a crazy preacher! Suddenly I heard my true preaching voice! Here were the most clear and penetrating insights I could have imagined! It was like, "Ted, if you really want to preach, here are the words you need! Look no further! This is what you've always wanted to say—to yourself, of course! These are the words you were seeking, when you were ten, yelling at the bushes and the birds! Here's the universal message: that Jesus can speak to the world through your own voice!" And so the voice went on and on, clearing from my brain the negative rhetoric around Jesus that I'd heard as a child, and that still permeates the Western Mind, whether people call themselves Christian or not. I wanted, then, to soak in the language of The Course; and what better way than to live with an official teacher of The Course, someone who lived ACIM from moment to moment.

****

To live with someone so dedicated to forgiveness and happiness was a great experiment. I grew to love the sensation that our conceptual world really is a nightmare—therefore, Not the Real World! Here is the joke called irony. To understand, conceptually, that it's not necessary to look into the past or the future for truth. What a happy idea: to recognize that the past never happened, that whatever I may have thought Dad did, could really be seen as the product of a mental nightmare, including my own troubled existence! The separation is not real: it is the journey of The Son of God, coming to re-member the Home he never left! We return to the Earth again as though for the first time. The self within you makes this material and prodigal journey through space/time.

In Hinduism, the end is obscure, and in The Prodigal

story, there's still the problem of the resentful brother. Now I wanted to see the innocent truth in every other being, so that all the obstacles to seeing—truth—could be found in my own mind—for correction! If I can see you as Jesus in the flesh, it doesn't matter what you do, I'm the one responsible for seeing correctly! I need not believe in your nightmare/reality! I need not take men at War seriously, but as dreaming—their mind in a real nightmare!

I was discovering the reconciliation of language systems. I'm a heretic, after all. I do see ACIM as an aspect of the pattern, and very useful for Human (Western) Mind Training. It is not required of HDS students to grasp the mysticism of the label: The Language Of The Maya. We are all ensconced in it, even the resurrected. It is not our will. For example, my body tells me to sleep alone, though when I was normal, I endured sleeping in the same bed with the same person every night, forever. That's an education in the power of conditioning. Those couples start looking like the same person. I now insist on sleeping alone, for the most part. Great to have some fun, but when it comes to sleeping, leave me alone! What anguish this was for Joy, who saw the purpose of relationship as joining at every level, the collapsing of all barriers for the sake of the blessed union of The Son. Yes, that's a very nice concept, now leave me alone so I can rejuvenate in my own aura, and I'll meet you fresh as a daisy in the morning! Joy never could get used to me going off to my own bed, which I always did after getting up to pee sometime in the night. She'd sometimes sneak into my bed, and I'd have to drive her away. We'd laugh about it too.

She was also a student of the "Byron Katie Work;" and I provided her many a "Judge Your Neighbor" worksheet. It was impressive how she kept working through her thoughts and feelings around my weak, though unapologetic, ego. I would do or say something, challenging the clarity of her happiness, and she'd plunge straight off her abstract cliff into suicidal despair. Even a perfect person may shove you toward the stairs, or whisper "evil" evilly at night. My tribal ego took each occurrence, of her rushing off mad, as a shot to the heart. Where did you go? I was just getting started! My feelings take some time, ratcheting up on waves, up to that (delicious) height of really letting loose on the hateful side of love—O, the burden of love!

Yet "The Work" did wonders for Joy. I was really impressed. She would storm off to her room and slam the door, like it was the end of the world—to me. Then she'd emerge, hours later, skipping like a little goat, prancing around in a fit of happiness! It was pure alchemy. She wouldn't let herself leave her room until she'd attained a breakthrough: until she could let *me* off the hook of her anger and frustration. When she finally did burst back out of her room, and did her little dance, she made me sit while she read from her Judge Your Neighbor Worksheet.

The first part of the Judge Your Neighbor Worksheet gives you permission to have a controlled temper tantrum—keeping the punch line hidden. She did this with the mental acuity of scientific analysis, tearing the fabric of my being to shreds, only to turn it all completely around, convincing me in the end that the whole episode had absolutely nothing to do with me. She wanted me to see how some ancient wound in herself (so of all humanity), some egoic shortsightedness on her part, had simply prevented her from seeing me just as I am: the holy Son of God, innocent in all respects! I couldn't believe it! At the end of her process she had recognized what a thoughtful listener I was after all! All I ever had to do was exercise a little patience, and listen with attention to her process.

I strongly encourage anyone talking about Jesus to please read ACIM for a year—and clear the repulsive image out of your mind! Now I want to say to my White Christian World (today!): See Jesus!—stop looking for Jesus—dumb ass! Or, the Western-Christian-State-version-of-Jesus, that you worship, is just a killer monkey! You should hate what's become of Jesus! Perhaps this is my jihad.

In the end I was defenseless to love. We even broke up in love! It was the sweetest heartbreak in the world. I have never cried so hard and freely. To part, in the knowledge that the separation is not real, was a lesson in eternity. Once we established the knowledge of that metaphysical connection, as the truth of who We Really Are, all the problems seemed a bit silly, even though we had to go through all of them. She taught me never to doubt the reality of love. We are all a bit crazy, but we can't blame ourselves: that would perpetuate the nightmare. We really each need understanding. In other words: The Jews and the Palestinians do not understand how deeply they love each other! Those deadly and seemingly interminable hatreds, humankind has always known, cannot be taken as the final word on the truth within each of us. We can see through the nightmare, and remember, the one who holds us all together in the illusion of our separation, is ever One.

And/But the Son of God is in a state where he does not remember to laugh. He takes the world seriously and fails to recognize the illusion for what it is. How can a serious person really help you with your "problems"?! We can experience all the lessons, along the way, as teaching us to see through the veil, and to remember Who We really are.

Everything that happens to me now helps me to see my own blocks to love. Byron Katie still had to learn. Be kind to the body. But Blame is the overriding energy that will sacrifice the body to its cause. When we feel entitled to blame, we strike, we kill. Blame, the chemistry that keeps us locked into the nightmare (literally), must be undone in my own life! You can't blame yourself or others when you see "the world" (the conceptual background) to be a nightmare perpetuated BY blame. My story exists in the universal theme of all humanity: what will you do with blame? We must overcome it—beneath the dome of one skull at a time.

Joy was an unbelievable teacher. Now I recommend ACIM for all normal Christians. It's time to wipe the idol of "The Lord Jesus," depicted as the repulsive image on the cross, and replace it with Who You Really Are: The Son of God within you. These words are for Western Christian understanding! When they get this, it won't matter what other people believe. Why should a true follower of Jesus care about what others believe? See All In Christ—the end!

****

I experienced another practical shift in my consciousness while living with Joy. I was asking myself, since I can't be an atheist, how am I now to experience my relationship with God? One day, the answer came: Comedy! StandUp Comedy! If there is a God, then God must be my Stand-Up Comedy Coach! I got Obsessed with humor, and Standup comedy, I thought, now I've finally found my real calling! I had read somewhere, that America brings (only) these three gifts to the world (universally): Jazz (from Black people), The Twelve-Step Program, and StandUp Comedy!

Like trying to learn how to become a professional "spenger" on the streets of Victoria, I got to work learning everything I could about the history of Humor and Stand-Up Comedy. I ordered about twenty books, and more from the library: historical, philosophical, and practical manuals on how to do Stand Up. I hired a coach! I took a whole semester class on Stand-Up Comedy at the community college. I listened to 103 FM—all the time. I bought a little recorder, which I used when a joke came to me. Pretty soon I filled a whole binder with jokes. I practiced at The Comedy Club in Denver, and at a little bar on Colfax, I forget the name. It was down the street from The Squire, where mostly Black comedians did their thing. I was told it would be way too rough for me.

I bombed at StandUp (see Appendix #3), every time, badly.

I've heard the most awful silence(s) in the world; painful gig-gles are no better, maybe worse. At least the silence could be interpreted as "spiritual." Once, a comedian following me, wished he could just beat me up. I can tell you, bombing is the most humiliating thing a human being can experience. It was worse than going to the blackboard in grade school.

I could imagine the funniest routines, and I hear crowds of people laughing in my head. So when I kept bombing at StandUp, I actually felt betrayed by God. If God is a comedy coach, Her seduction is, originally, convincing; sinister really. She gave me funny routines, and even provided an ecstatic audience who loved me... and it was all in my mind! I really thought I could make people crack up and laugh. But then, when the real thing happens... nothing, a dreadful silence, or that one desperate nervous giggle! Now that's a room full of very awake, and, very awkward people—every single one of them! "Bombing" is a riveting moment, indeed a poignant bardo, for everyone present. I can tell you, for the one tell-ing the jokes—that's a bad feeling! I was not consoled by the knowledge that so many great comedians had bombed in their early careers. Well my sensitivity to failure must be more acute. Like spenging... I really thought *that* would be a piece of cake. Just sit there and people will give you money. No, just sit there and feel people looking down on you. Just sit there and feel like shit, a failure, jealous that people on the sidewalk can walk into any store and buy things. No. Bombing at StandUp is the worst; and unless I can find a way in, by accident, forget it. I won't go through that again.

****

I don't know if I felt driven to atheism, but I think I fired God as my StandUp comedy coach. OK, I do think it's a good theory. I hired God to be my Stand-Up coach, in general life, because I really do think that until I can find a way to laugh about my experiences, I have not seen them correctly. I hold on to that. I know there are a lot of terrifying things going on in the world... awful scenes of torture and child abuse. Humans who seem to enjoy hurting other humans. Monsanto... oppressive governments... making better bombs... a lot of things that piss me off and make me want to scream! It's hard for me to laugh about what we're doing to the earth; the disruption of the "natural order" and the destruction of the lifestyles of those who have lived in harmony with the earth... it just makes me want to cry, and put those high ranking colonialists, of the Babylonian System (my people), down in front of me for a tongue lashing... My mind-training tells me I would just be yelling at myself. HDS tells me that there's a Program; we really don't control anything; everything is unfolding as it should; no choice; wait and see; love yourself—there is nothing else.

I take the high road, anyway. I think I have to see this world from a perspective that's not just locked into the battle-ground. The relentless appeal to yet more pain, as though proof that there is something terribly real going on... we've got to question that archaic thinking today. When I say this is a dream, and you say, "No, let me tell you about what some guy did to this little girl—now you tell me that's not serious! I'll kick you!—tell me that's a dream!" But is it not the case, that the worse we see things, the more insane we are in our thinking?

We CAN CHANGE OUR MINDS! The "Holocaust" and the mussel manners, and Hannah Arendt's research, all those wheelchairs, Saddam becomes ISIS... not in a straight line, but through our progressive building up in the predictable dynamics of the nightmare: memetic violence! We have the anthropology and the science to prove, we tend to have this problem with violence. And we've had it, as a serious problem, from just before agriculture and the building of cities. We always face our worst fears. And isn't it time we stand and pause for a moment, and just take a look at what We've done? With tears. OK, so I can't quite laugh yet. But I want to. I want to be willing to find the whole world of Man a huge joke—we Can wake up from—within. The Nightmare is the joke! Isn't it kinder and easier to wake up!—than that we continue to insist on how real (we think) it is; how serious, so ensuring the very negativity we try to overcome, with our commitment to eternal violence? ACIM tells us that we can correct a mental mistake, but never a real sin. We have mental problems, period. It's our tole in The Totality.

****

Joy found my ego a little too extreme and unruly. One of the ways I had come to express myself was to dance at bars, in front of live bands. After eighteen years, Dance Home had folded. Recently, it has been revived, but for a few years I didn't have a regular "spiritual" dance practice... so I made the best of it and went to the bars, and started "swirling" in front of the bands. That's fun... also risky. People haven't seen that... a guy wearing plastic shoes, whirling like a top, nonstop, inches from the mics. I'm challenged by the edge of things. So while I was living with Joy, on Saturday nights, I would walk to a bar at the most western edge of the downtown strip, make my way from bar to bar, drink a beer fast, and spin, leave, drink a beer and spin... I could make it through four or five bars like that.

I guess one night, someone must have called the cops. I don't know. I had finished my routine and was walking home, almost there, enjoying the stillness of the night. So, while whirling my way across a deserted street, two cop cars pulled up suddenly and, without conversation, started to arrest me. Now I'm a pretty skillful contact dancer, so the feel of their hands on me, in my drunken state, was simply an invitation to dance. They were strong guys though, with unforgiving movements. Still, it took quite a few delicious moments, with me sliding all over the place, until they finally hoisted me into the air and planted me face down on top of the cruiser.

Of course it didn't hurt at all, and actually felt really satisfying. The timing of the impact perfectly spread from my torso to the side of my face. Ah, how skillfully done—these are real cop moves. I was consciously impressed, I mean, it could have been my nose that struck the roof first. Still, I was provoked at that point, and proceeded to preach at the cops. They said "Wow" as we got to the station.

I kept it up from my cell, where I sang, and had a chance to practice, full bore, my researched lecture on a certain negative stream in American history. What happened with the Puritans? Are we still seeking revenge against the tribe and calling "them" terrorists? Lincoln... is this now a Police state? Wilson... are we exporting this to the world? You don't really know who I am... You descend from on high and lay down the letter of the law! Do I have no local value to you? My artful performance means nothing?! Is this how we treat local people everywhere on the earth? Do humans get no respect now?

Reagan! Who benefits from my stay in your jail? Do you know who I know? Bush! What kind of lawless world do we live in now? What have I done? No phone call? Am I part of some experiment: what will normal people do when you lock them up for no good reason!? Do you know there's a woman right now who's worried sick about me? Really, you no longer allow a phone call? What's happening to America? Four hours of preaching later, one of the officers out in the main area said, "You're making me want to jump off a very tall building." That made me think of Alleluia, jumping off the roof for Jesus. Good. That was enough.

They let me out in the morning without saying a word, or asking me to pay for the night in their hotel. They finally let me call Joy, who came right away and picked me up. I don't know what it was for, but the enrichment of my personal experience/journey.

****

When I moved back, once again, to Boulder, I continued on the momentum of going to a Reggae bar to dance. I also started attending a poetry open mic regularly. So back in March, 2014, driving from the poetry open mic to the Outback, I pulled into a parking spot, and was about to get out of my car when a female police officer walked up and asked to see my ID, and all that stuff. I didn't know what was going on, but I'd had a Vodka and tonic at the previous bar two hours before. Two more cop cars appeared suddenly. When they asked me to get out of the car and walk toward them... I had to spin around a few time. "First mistake. Same experience. The police report said that I was reaching for them "erotically." Well, if you reach to grab me when I'm drunk, yeah!... Once they had me in the car, a Latino cop in training asked me to choose between a breath test, or a blood test. I answered that I lived under the philosophy of No Choice. He insisted that I would have to choose. I begged to differ: "No Choice—is this a choice for me, really?"

He said, "If that's your choice, we'll take it as a refusal." Second mistake, and a more serious sentence.

A DUI, whatever the circumstances, is yet another extreme experience for which I am now grateful. I gave up my car, and I've been riding a bike for a year or more. I quit drinking, what little I did, and smoking pot, which might have been more. I'm happy for the break. There are a lot of things I won't do unless I have to.

The other thing is, people have been encouraging me to write this story. But I've been way too busy—dancing, performing, and writing poetry—to take the time to write the whole thing out. Now the time is forced upon me, like the will of Allah. What's your story? I'm also trying to study sentences and paragraphs and grammar, but as you can see, I'm not making much progress. Those subjects, and math, terrified me in school. I'm still trying to overcome my fears.

Anyway, I know it's late and time for bed. Hey! As far as I can tell (you) I'm In The Most Exciting Story Going On! Come On!

Appendix #1

Adam and Eve: What Really Happened

If my professor was asking us to imagine Adam seeing Eve naked for the first time, then he would have been asking about human experience after The Fall. Unless he wanted us to, merely, view a naked woman as an animal would: without human desire, or lust. However, this was no mere animal, Adam. But I wanted to know: what sort of event could have turned a Neanderthal(?) into A Man?

My research into "The Fall" brought forward three essential ingredients. 1) a talking female; 2) a magic mushroom; 3) and a "blow job." I mean, we're talking about sin here, so don't be surprised by these references. So Eve (could have been Lilith) approaches Adam, sits him down against a tree, and offers her—soon to become Man—a magic mushroom. She asks him to wait, where he is. As the effects of the schrooms begin to work, Eve comes back through the bushes, across from him. She parts the leaves and moves toward him erotically, where he sits leaning back comfortably against the tree. She talks to him, calls him by name, and then does something he has never experienced before—oral sex. Now, the combination of 1) speech, (2) the effects of chemistry on the mind, and 3) pornographic sex—changed (at least contributed to the change) of the animal—into the Man! And to this day, Man's basic problems are linguistic confusion, meaningless sex, and the

219

use of drugs and alcohol—medicine for the human condition.

The "Fall fantasy" I'd had in Bible College didn't get very far. Eve, naked, parting the leaves; Adam, a stunned look on his face. Now what would my Bible College professor think about a talking female, a magic mushroom, and a blow job? Biblical Realism? He say, "Use your imaginations!"

Appendix #2

The Gathering of Dogmas

I came to see, that each of the ten stages of the Prenatal Sequence could be read in ten institutionalized religions. In other words, there are ten religions, in my/your body, which I project out in the world as ten different world religions. It all begins and ends with The Throat Center, with Manifestation—where everything is pouring out into the World/Maya. This is literally everything about speech and gestures and expression—and the "real" world appearing all around us now. And so, we come to the Story of Israel.

I

I give the first dimension, the first stage in the sequence (The Throat), to the Hebrew people. Can I say Jewish People? Well, the first of the Abrahamic Brothers, anyway. These religious people are here to talk—to tell a story—and to keep the story interesting. And the way they're telling that story today is frightfully boring, a repetitious killer-monkey-onto-action. We have to hate it. Not the people, the sick story the Zionists are telling!

So here's my version of "the most interesting story!" If I could make a call to Israel, I'd shout out, "Call The Rainbow

Gathering to Israel! Give up your obsession for a piece of land, and remember Israel, in the end, is the Voice for All humanity! No longer: Our special land; Our special book; Our special people; Our separate God: but Welcome Home Friend!" This is my version of American Zionism! It's my story, as a distant cousin of the Jews (I inherited my middle name, Leavitt, from Jewish ancestors on my father's side. I really am just a messenger, after all).

Another lesson I learned from the Human Design System about the "Throat Center," was that our relationship to The Story is both micro and macro. At the macro level: Israel = Welcome Home Earth—the last chapter! And at the micro level, it means we each have a story to tell. Today each of us is The Messiah—and we can say that, because Ra Uru Hu proclaimed, with evidence: Love Yourself! Furthermore, a Story is never true; but it has to be interesting—more interesting than the story the Jews are telling today! Israel today is such a boring story, reeks of hell, as meaningless as Auschwitz, and as meaningless as a nursing home in White America! Can we keep the Palestinians in a ghetto forever?

Meanwhile, in a more interesting Story, the Palestinian Area is The Sacred Site, including the Mosque! (Sometimes I see a crystal see-through Temple protecting The Masjid Inside.) Makkah, it follows, must be the spiritual Trade Circle for the Global Permaculture Economy on Earth. Yeah, Baby, it's an American Style Rainbow Gathering, after all! Now come on dude—THAT's an interesting Story—and it's happening everywhere on planet Earth today! I'm telling you, this is a super retro whatever virus that won't be stopped!

My enthusiasm for The Gathering (my connection to Israel) is over-the-top; I realize—delusional. So I'll reiterate. When the meaning of "Israel" becomes, simply: *the location (A Camp) for Global Gathering*, then perhaps all our religious problems might have a chance for resolution. The meaning of Israel is, surely, derived from a culture of people who claim a Book for their Reality. If the meaning of "Israel" is "Story!" then it has to be an interesting Story—and it has to be interesting for everyone, the entire world!—or it's going to have a bad ending, once again! And The Trade Circle?: means Family, means Islam, means Permaculture! But I'd have to insert an essay: "On The Meaning of Islam: Permaculture Economy!" And I do consider it the Will of Allah—to make it so on earth!

II

In the second chapter, I remind myself to quit looking for some transcendental Home in a life beyond time and space. Earth is the only Home I need to know. I give up seeking any other Paradise. (What we call The Afterlife pertains to The Erron, of HDS, but that's another story!). Looking for Paradise is a joke when you realize you never left... Home! Earth! In the second stage, we address the issue of Space. The Universe seems to be contained in the Space (the displacement of Time and Space) around the event of The Big Bang. Here, I turn to the Gnostics—throughout human history—to provide an overall context in our World: for the emphasis on the Individual who must come to terms with, and become responsible for... the conceptual error in the mind of Sophia/Wisdom! What is Wisdom/Sophia, after all, but an education in the restoration of innocence; innocence, lost perhaps in a Conceptual Mistake? What is the transition from innocence-to-shame-to-innocence but an event in The Mind?

It was the male—God of the Patriarchy—who claimed to be the Creator of our World and who demanded allegiance in the mind of Man. The Jewish God is of The Story and Language In (All Things) Conversation; the Christian God is the singularity of The Friend (in your own sternum!) in the healing of memetic violence; and the Muslim Allah is The Force for Permaculture on Earth—for real! For Now! This will create a voice for global economy, and manifest in Israel, Sacred

Palestinian area, Mecca area Trade Circle. But in the old telling of our story, The Gnostic God is a terrible reminder to us, of what happens when we give authority to our own inner Thinking—at the expense of The Body. We grow serious! The two first brothers rule by mental-dominance-technology, and the third reacts with physical terror. The same. It's Time to Understand this conflict, and stop it.

The world was conceived in error—for which we have always blamed the feminine. Recapitulated in the story of The Fall, the feminine always bears the brunt of Man's problems with language, with chemistry, and with meaningless sex. The Gnostics are the heretics of every age. Joseph Smith—perhaps the greatest example (though you shouldn't believe such a person) of White American uniqueness. This piece of writing is my Gnostic offering. I throw it into Space. If this section is confusing, that's how Gnosticism works.

III

In the third chapter, I remind and empower the language of Hinduism with its fixation on the nature of the human Self. The Hindus teach us that the World itself, per se, is Maya—sheer illusion. How can the truth be known if all is unreal—already? Hinduism opens up a point for God in the dispassionate nature of The Friend, in the Way of The Friend: Krishna. There is only one true friend in the world—within you! Precisely located in the sternum, the Magnetic Monopole holds everything together in the illusion of separation. There's a well-known legend that Jesus went to India, where he learned from, and identified with, the Hindu concept of The Self, then integrated this "truth" within Judaism. That's what makes Jesus The Messiah, in that very fusion between the Throat Center and The G Center, between the Word and Identity. The friend within you is the similitude of The One, opening the way to the direct inner knowledge of the Unknowable God. Remember that every single thing in The Universe is held together by the Magnetic Monopole, rendering the fact both mundane and transcendent. Each of us is...

IV

In the fourth chapter, I surprise everyone, starting with myself. I turn Western Philosophy into a weird kind of Religion. "The Gathering Dogma" is *about* Religion, after all. (The about is what's important—for us to know) The whole of Western Philosophy reveals the nature of The Ajna Center itself, and its continued unfolding function (merely) To Think and Think.... Again. What is consciousness thinking? I'll argue that Western Philosophy, from Socrates and company to Rene Girard and Francois Laruelle, expresses Human Thinking, the nature of human thinking.

However, the profound danger—to human thinking—is the authority we give to the mind; imagining thinking capable of action. Wrong. May Socrates' death not be in vain! The Ajna Center, the center of Conceptualization, marks the true purpose of Man. Man is a Philosopher by definition! Earth is located where conscious thought (for The Totality) is emerging! And Man's essential problem, as a Philosopher, is with Religion! Mans real work (like this book about the Patriarchy) is that of a Philosopher. And as a Philosopher, he must differentiate Thinking from Religion. The Philosophers work, an intellectual work, is to reflect on how the Institutes Of Religion, and to show how they become negative when abstracted from The Body: when the Aspect is viewed as The Whole. Philosophy, thus envisioned, will safeguard against the human tendency to give authority to The Mind. In other words, repent: think again....

This is how Religion becomes "a bloody business" (said

Ra). When religion comes into conflict, we see the systems of the body (itself) in conflict. No wonder we're sick—but this is not required! (Because) We can now understand the function of religion within each human body—but only to Understand It!

My favorite researches were of Western Philosophy (a relentless dialectic/a progressive conversation), slowly developing a sense for how each philosopher fixates (their reflection) on a different center/stage of prenatal development: Here's my suggested, "Philosophy Curriculum (Read each of these philosophers in Sequence, and you will exercise your human mind): Socrates (with Plato and Aristotle), Francois Laruelle (NonPhilosophy (read quickly, and just for a sense of how Laruelle *uses* philosophy: be dazzled by what you can understand), Spinoza, Descartes, Nietzsche, Merleau-Ponty, Kant, Hegel, Ortega y Gesset, and Derrida.

It's only with the mind (after all) that we can both "make" mistakes and also "correct" mistakes. The mind can deal with the idea of a conceptual/perceptual error—prior to any material consequence. Mental mistakes can be fixed. Mistakes we act on become "serious," and require the extraction of a narrative: time/space "creation." An emotional mistake requires time/space for correction! There is an atonement. The human miracle is the creation of a being that can use his mind (speech/thinking/writing/reading) to change his mind.

I say, with A Course In Miracles: "Thank God I was wrong!" There is nothing to change, but our thinking (and even that—change—simply happens when it does, not because; we are in-formed). Everything good and bad flows from how We Think. From our conceptual error, the ego emerged, along with seriousness, sin, war, and blame—whatever we think our "problem" is. All of that negativity is attached to the Human Story. And when we experience changing our mind with our mind, we do not simply end our identification-with-identification—illusion, but we have the chance to shift our experience from The Nightmare to The Happy Dream. This is our illusion of choice. Choice got us here, and choice will bring us home: No Choice! (for those with ears).

V

Writing the fifth chapter made me nervous. The passions of The Ego... are not well understood, to say the least. Research led me to the conclusion that The Ego Center is reflected, in our world, through Islam, which makes Allah the only God The Ego can accept: The One-We God. We are all ego beings, after all! We were all born Muslims. If there is a single word that needs clarification in our world, it's the word "Ego." I have thought this through to a very happy conclusion; so before you read this and lose your mind, relax. We can work this linguistic mess through to completion. We have linguistic problems, before we have Ego problems.

How has America, the current dominant power in the world, inherited this theme—from all time? How do we now live out the conceptual error in which Man is ensconced and implicated? There is no need to look back through time to see how negativity works; though this will be revealed in time. It's working now. In my life. In every life. And the mistake is exemplified in the Systems of The World—which we mistakenly project, as merely "out there." These Systems of the World won't change until a statistically significant percentage of human beings have their minds restored to sanity and self love—as individuals.

Every good story involves a problem, and the hope of resolution. Maybe it all started great, but something happened, some negativity—to overcome—, some life-threatening challenge to face—and a cliff-hanger at the end. Reading led me to an interrogation of my own tradition—inherited from The British (the British East India Company BEIC, precisely).

The American problematic began when The Puritans

acted in revenge against Chief Potawa. They could not forgive, their own thoughts against "that Antichrist," "for it
must have been he who slaughtered Sir Walter Raleigh's crew."
As it turns out, Chief Potawa probably did meet Sir Walter
Raleigh's band of volunteers; and did in fact help the band
of losers. With the kind help of Chief Potowa, they very soon
established a perfectly functional, thriving, "Indian Village."
No sooner done than Chief Potowa,or Chief Seattle, had his
famous dream: White people coming in droves, destroying the
world in front of them. Not on his watch. He massacred the
little band of English villagers; the first, and last, White Indian
Village. There's a legend that two or three men escaped into
the wilderness. I think they're still on the run.

So the first spiritual act, of White American Protestantism,
was to take revenge upon themselves—the very thing the
"Jesus Event" no longer required. Consider the human ritual for blood sacrifice—and war. Is America not founded on
a kind of spiritual secret: the separation of mundane Local
Culture from God and State? The separation of earth and
heaven? The denigration of the earth in pursuit of heaven?
The Black (Body) slave and the White (Mind) master? But My
Wasp American Zionist Story is not done.

The second step (in this negative development) occurred
when Lincoln institutionalized The State—at the *expense* of
Local Culture—as the foundation of human growth and development. A State (Capitalist or Communist) would now become
the foundation for human social existence. Hence, local culture is only useful when it functions as a slave to the Power
of The State.

President Wilson, third step, turned the idealism of The
Nation State into a Global agenda, justifying a cause for endless war in the cause of Capitalism (God and State). Reagan,
furthermore, transformed the global economic system, giving
corporations authority over local culture and, individual freedom. The very Meaning, for all of humanity, would connect

the American Dollar to Oil and Gas (in your mind). Finally, the whole mistake is materialized in the Lawlessness of a single individual, when given power by The State—to rule the world. We now exist in a world where a single individual is given the illusion of authority, to do whatever he wants to do whenever he wants to do it. No individual in the history of the world, prior to America, has ever known what that could be! Call it "Mission Accomplished." [Written pre-Trump] No, call him Biden... call him Trump? Are we not about to find out?

Given the triumph of this form of Collective idealism— the destruction of local culture everywhere on planet Earth—I make an argument for the legitimacy of tribal terrorism, and making sense of the (sad) evil of Nationalism. When the human tribal ego is threatened, humanity feels threatened. Human ego beings, all of us, feel threatened these days. Terror wants you to rethink something; as when someone commits suicide—it makes you think again. Terrorism makes sense from a human/ego/tribal point of view. You don't lock people up and torture them and then demand a level playing field.

And Nationalism is but the dispersion of the human Tribe, when all that's left is The State. The American South was not a Democracy. Slavery happens when The (Christian) State dominates The (Islamic) Tribe. The Human Heart! Nationalism has no roots on the ground. Therefore, it becomes an expression of (what we think of as) evil. It's not real, it's the negative spirit of the human tribe in the guise of "national specialness:" it's the Corporation, and Satanism.

Acts of disorder are but proof that disorder exists. In a parallel sense, Homo sapiens, as individuals, are designed to be suicidal when their fundamental sense of meaning in this world is threatened. So we are in no position to blame terrorists, and further, use their terrorism as a pretext for destroying their Tribal Way of Life. For example: While Hamas behaves as a form of institutionalized terrorism, we cannot expect them to behave any differently, while the Jewish State, with the support of American Collective/State idealism, secretly employs their own institutionalized hatred against Islam! Think about it: How can the American "Jesus" accept and celebrate the Islamic world?

The State, in the end, exists to Serve all Life (not only Local culture) on Planet Earth! The State exists to provide services and oversight for the needs of the global Permaculture economy! So the terrorist is really a child in need, screaming for help; and it doesn't help to beat the child for crying and screaming! People need food. And shelter. And clothing. Or they will break down Macy's and vandalize the facade. Martyrs of Islam will yet be called on to march toward the guns in the name of Allah. But not without the Christians who re-member their true martyrs (the AntiWar movement) of the early Church. Wait and See. A colorful army is coming.

VI

In the sixth chapter, I make the case for African and Native Spiritualities, outward expressions of The Human Splenic System. How We all think about Africa is—how we all think—about "having bodies!" As far as I can tell, the human body is in the condition of an Afropessimist!—Don't expect "dumb ass" to come Home! The Body of Humanity cannot rest until the White Prodigal hears the call: Come Home! There is no "great again" but the thrill of letting go, of returning to our senses. WASP American Zionists have a chance to actually Be The Prodigal—in the pig sty! Let's go Home bro! Enough of this shit! Enough of this colonization of our own Body! And anyway... it seems up to us, after all!

VII

In chapter seven, I argue that China represents the Foundation of The Human Condition. China is like physics, or poetry. In other words, China gives expressions to real (mundane) human interests and, furthermore, what it takes to make those interests real. Do we value war? They show us how to fight. Do We value structure—above all? Mao Tse Tung. Do We value money above Everything? Then we'll make the biggest dams and factories in the world. I get a thrill, imagining 800 million Han in a coordinated Tai Chi flow. Our world has a foundation, as sure as stress and adrenaline. We build on that. The Chinese can harness the stress tension/energy, of human interest, on a huge scale. But for what? We have to ask ourselves now: What does Humanity really want? Here's my answer: when China re-members the requirement for Permaculture Based Economy, We may experience the healing of The Body on Planet Earth! Imagine all those Chinese, forced into cities, now encouraged to return Home (given a choice) to their gardens—and create models for a Permaculture Economy. They will be doing the Will of Allah!

VIII

Chapter Eight brings us to the Solar Plexus and the emergence of The Breath, the emerging focus for human spiritual life on planet Earth today.

The seeds for my personal research into The Breath began in the time period after first meeting Ra. One day, I was squatting barefoot beside the Boulder Creek, taking a break "prayer time" on my walkabout, when I found myself gazing at my feet as though for the first time. I thought, omg, The Feet express Mr. Gurdjieff's Law of Seven—in the flesh! I find it hard to believe that I'm the only person to have seen Gurdjieff in my feet! It's plain to see! I had seen the Law of Seven, mentally, but no one pointed at my feet!

The map of my feet became a literal portal into another world, a spiritual world. The stages of learning were many, and it's weird—trying to describe my process. For a long time all I could do was stand there at arm's length and marvel at the portal/window. Applying the law of seven to my balance, my mind could grasp, in real time, the past, the present/balance, and the future, relative to the points and lines in the law of seven—in the feet!

I practiced moving my balance around, based on the six basic points, the heels and the two points ahead on each foot. I would always be aware of which point my balance was on, which point I had come from, and which point I was moving my balance toward. The past, the present, the future... under the feet! That's a wow!—for me. I started to imagine my feet as neutrino surfboards. What I had learned while standing, really took off when I applied it to running. It's exciting, and new every time. Climb into your chariots, my people!

For three years, I'd been mapping, gazing, and balancing along the points and lines suggested by the internal feet enneagram, and the star pattern around the feet, when something happened that literally bounced me out of my standing position. The separate points and lines joined in a surging force and shoved me away from the wall. I'd been feeling a weird kind of fear; a kind of pulse, like an electrical buzz, as when approaching an energy source. It was as though I were on a tightrope over the Grand Canyon—and might fall! I'd had no previous sense for the space under my feet. And here I'd been walking around all my life—since I first stood up—as though I knew what I was doing! It felt like a joke... all this philosophy—and I can't tell you the mechanics of how we manage to stand up!—never mind walk around! How does the balance really go from the heel to the front of the foot... or from the heel to the base of the baby toe on the other side, and back?

A further, disconcerting, awareness arose as I noticed the very sexy curves under my feet. Sure, the mind can deal with points and lines, but the body doesn't "do" points and lines! It

232

curves and swirls around. I was certainly not expecting to find in my feet such blatant sexual imagery.

I had found a cross: the vertical—slash dividing the feet—, and the horizontal line that connects at the base of the baby toes. The Cross—it's right there! Is there not a geometry of The Cross at the base of any building program? Place a square, point down (the balance point) on the vertical line, and connect the forty-five-degree angle to the points at the base of the baby toes. Using the horizontal line (from baby toe to baby toe—the same as a comfortable hand span) for the radius, you can draw a circle around your feet. What you see is the mandala for The Human Design System with its two wheels (Astrological and I Ching) and the Body Graf in the center.

The image of the cross (prior to this vision) could evoke nothing but that gruesome image. We can still see it, in any Roman Catholic Church, looking down on us and taunting the imagination with horror. I call that image "the repulsive image." The seemingly dead body of Jesus on the Cross, invisible, there, in the background. It's obvious, and I couldn't deny it.

And I continue to consider the image of Jesus on the cross to be the most profound icon (for human contemplation) on the problem of re-sentiment. It's the only image I know that can deal directly with this ancient human retro-virus: sheer negativity. Who do you blame, right now? But "Jesus" means: "Sacrifice is no longer required!" Our sacrificial system just is The Nightmare! It is not required. We can wake up, but only when we first understand The Nightmare, in which our minds are ensconced. The Nightmare is perpetuated—in each mind—by the requirement of blame (a real energy), the placing of blame to ensure that justice is done.

The diseased serum, to "kill all the enemy," can never be applied to The Body. The end of the mind game is the end of blame, the end of the religious story, and the completion of Man in restoration of The Feminine Body. I really do think, when the Christian world wakes up to the joke, that sacrifice is no longer required—love yourself—they will put an end to war, there will be peace on earth. We don't have to be fucked up forever people. To follow Jesus is to let every being off the hook. You don't have to be friendly—just kill all your own enemies first—under the dome of your own skull!

It was another friend, Christopher, who pointed out to me, how, if you put the tips of your index fingers at the meeting of the vertical and horizontal lines (the cross in the feet), and your thumbs at the meeting of the heels, mirrored in each hand, you can see the clear outline of a female body from neck to ankle. When you trace your hands on the feet, there is no longer a cross and a dying man, but the clear impression of the essential feminine form! I call that image the resurrection, for it appears over the "Repulsive (pornographic) Image" that continues to inspire the Christian world today. I would encourage them to look through their own feet and hands for the proper pornography, pointing to the experience we really want: To Resurrect: To Stand Up! So, I say, take your pick of images for The Cross: the repulsive male image of the dying god—you must still imagine—or the female image, discovered in the form itself: In your hands. You have your own cross to bear.

There's an even more troubling image (I could not avoid noticing!); it's downright pornographic, in fact, it's a "cum shot," one for each foot. So the male is the binary. Notice the "jade stalk," in each foot, from the outside of the heel to the tip at the base of the baby toes, and the ejaculation—the toes depict from the small to the increasingly large—drops. But I'll leave that to your own imagination—it's all in your feet, after all. Look again. Repent.

Besides standing-breath-work, I gradually learned, through walking and running, how to bind the static standing pattern to the movement of the feet. Running introduced me to the discovery of breathing gears. Besides breathing the star pattern, for which the feet are the core, breathing in four counts and breathing out eight, or along the five lines of the star, counting 3,3,3,4,4 (or whatever). The Law of Seven showed me quite a few patterns. I would find a pattern and stick with it for months. This was my reason for running: I was learning to fly! Hey, grandpa AI!

A day would eventually come when I'd imagine shifting the direction of the breath pattern—and once I saw it, I'd have to let go of the old gear and ease into the fresh pattern. It would take two or three days for the visual pattern to adjust, training the breath how to move through most efficiently. I'm sure I experimented with twenty different patterns/gears, each for weeks, months and years at a time. I've been in a "five breath" pattern—following the star under the feet—for at least a year now. I don't know how it looks to others, but it's not normal movement; it's pretend flying!

IX

Pressing on to the ninth chapter. I see a Movement arising from Eastern Russia, expressing the biology of life among us and restoring the meaning of the true power of The State—when used to serve. Power used in the service of humanity is the proper functioning of The State, Capitalist (Splenic) or Communist (Solar Plexus). We may see the full manifestation of this power, sometime between 2060 and 2065, and it makes a weird sense in the HDS precession. Newton points to this date in his own calculations for the return of Christ. But The Rainbow are not waiting for any One to return: We Are The One We've Been Waiting For! Let your I become We with The Rainbow Gathering, and you will See The Messiah!

X

Finally. The Silence. The Buddha. See through the eyes of The Passenger. The work of Man is complete in a kind of mathematical clarity. Mathematics provides the supreme inspiration for The Mind. Mathematical requirements pressure the mind to clarify its confusions, doubts, and mysteries—with formulaic clarity. In this way the Mind really is dominated by The Question. We are Questioned. We are that which is interrogated. We can say this now because HDS reveals to us, as human beings, precisely how we are integrated, with all nature, and all creation as we know it. We can each come to terms with the unique roles we play. Then we may experience the world as a piece of theater in which we are each an essential actor. Now we have our lines and can finally enjoy the drama—as ourselves! Without this knowledge, it's no wonder so many brilliant mathematicians have lost their minds at the outer limits of human comprehension. Math cannot take you beyond this limited world, but it can take you to the edge where no man has gone before. Math breaks down, like God, beyond knowledge. Wait and see; we will yet comprehend what we can understand. It's All Emptiness, It's All Full, No Choice Now.

Appendix #3

Comedy Routines (BA, failed)

So, I'll share with you all my "bombs." This is my memoir, not Stand-Up... yet. Wait and see.

I start off with a culturally neutral joke, something most people should be able to relate to.

New caregivers are not properly trained in performing peri-care. If peri-care (it turns out) is such a huge part of senior care, why is there not more training? Why do caregivers think of peri-care as the simple swish of a wet wipe, like the *signum crucis*? Because poop actually gets everywhere... down the legs, on the floor... it spreads around. New caregivers want to puke when they first encounter all that poop. A good training should prepare them for the worst! So, here, I suggest the real initiation into The World Of Caregiving.

The rules are simple.

Divide up in pairs, and take turns. Now, one of you, bear down and have a dump in your pants. It doesn't matter if it's large or small or medium sized, since you'll need to be prepared for all kinds of shit. Then walk around the room for a bit, get up on the hospital bed, roll to your tummy and back again. Lie there on your back. Then totally relax, and try to go to sleep. You may not help your partner, whose job it is to perform peri-care for you, and to clean up. We will be here to inspect your performance as it goes; and we'll be carrying buckets, in case you must vomit. Here are the supplies you'll need: gloves, chucks, towels, pans for warm water, washcloths, trash cans, toilet paper, and yes, wet wipes—lots of wet wipes!—also the perineal soaps, and barrier creams for anyone who's already developing a rash.

****

Now, what about "the greatest generation that ever lived"? What do they do when they need help? They dial 1-800 Ass Wipe. "Hi, I just went to the bathroom, and I can't reach back there to wipe myself anymore."... "No, no one is around to help me. I have three wonderful children. One's a doctor, one's a lawyer, and the other's on a yacht; right now he's sailing around the tip of South America! They don't have time. No, I don't know my neighbors. But I am very proud of my children, and we are a wonderful family... But that's mean, and kinda true cos it happens.

****

I prepared a few religious jokes. That may be where I lost people. You can talk about shit, but don't challenge belief.

My dad called my penis "Jonny." He taught me from day one: the proof of sin, original sin, is what happens to make Jonny stand up and demand your hand. You need to know, from early on, how the Devil (or Satan, they're all terribly evil) is knocking on the door through the very throb you can feel from Jonny! That throb is the definitive proof of original sin and your powerlessness to overcome it by your own willpower. Now, furthermore, your inability, in your own strength to resist Jonny, is proof that you need Jesus! And if you keep giving in to Jonny, that serpent, you'll end up fornicating and lascivious. You'll end up drunk in the gutter down an alley by the porn store. This is also not funny because it happens to too many believers.

****

My grandfather's name was Alleluia Irenaeus, and his brother's name was Ezekiel. They were raised in India as missionaries' kids themselves. As twenty-year-olds, they were reading the Bible and concluded that Jesus would return, but much sooner than anyone else had realized. And it says in the Bible, everyone on earth needed to be warned, first, before the event itself... and think of the thousands of villages in India who have never even heard the name "Jesus!" They would have to be warned! But how? The situation was so urgent, that, only by flying could they possibly reach the teeming millions. They prayed for an entire year, seeking faith to help them make the leap, and trust in God for the flight. God can perform miracles. When the year of prayer was complete, they climbed up on the roof, and after a final prayer meeting... jumped.

But can you imagine two white guys flying... into your village... only to announce: "Jesus is about to come? He doesn't have to flap his arms, the way we do—he'll burst through the air like Superman!"

****

Have you ever wondered what really happened at the famous "Fall of Man"? What really happened at "the original sin"? When you have been raised with that story, you begin to imagine it from every point of view you can... and I think I found the scene. It happened about eighty to ninety thousand years ago, somewhere in East Africa. First of all, it all started when a female had a mutation in her larynx that allowed her sacral sounds to be transformed into whatever we call speech. The dude she was with, let's call him Adam, did not know how to make those sounds. It was her mutation, not his. So obviously she had to teach him how to talk. That's the first thing to keep in mind. The second thing to understand is that the Neanderthal probably learned, from experience, to avoid eating the mushrooms: because some of them can kill you or make you sick, and otherwise do things that non-thinking beings would have no reason to eat them for.

Along with talking, Eve (though my version sounds more like Lilith here) must have started to Think. So she had found a mushroom that did something interesting to her mind. She becomes capable of fantasy. And that has something to do with our scene. So you have to imagine this. Here comes our babe through the woods... "Here Adam, come here sweetie... I have something for you... it's OK, it won't kill you, I've tried it... come on, it's OK, just eat this and you'll see. Now, lie back against this tree. I'm going to do something for you that will feel really good, and you can watch!" A talking female, a magic mushroom, and a blow job... that blew his circuitry... and Man has not recovered from the explosion of 1) Bla bla bla, and 2) drugs drugs drugs, and 3) blow job after blow job after fuck-ing blow job... Do you know that dudes (back in the day) spent more money on pornography (before the internet came along) than Hollywood and Nashville—combined?!

****

My missionary ancestors, always seeking to save the hea-then at the gates of hell, made it to Missouri only to find the Indians (there) welcomed them and helped them to survive. So they decided, the really bad Indians must come from India itself! India must be where the real heathen live; that must be the land of deepest darkness, indeed, teeming millions lost in sin! And my missionary grade school teachers could prove it!

"Look, children... look at the gods they worship here... this is why your parents do God's work, and why you have been left at Sunrise boarding school—so your parents have the time to save these lost souls, perishing on the brink of hell, worshipping the gods in these bloody pictures. I mean, look at the horrible gods they worship... like this female, for example, with her tongue all bloody, in her many hands, the heads and limbs of men she's ripped apart with her fangs... now take your eyes from such horror and idolatry and look over here upon the face of our Lord Jesus, there, on the cross... dying for you, yes you, because of your sins, and their sins... Jesus loves them too... see the thorns on his brow, his torn flesh, the blood pouring from his side... beautiful Lord Jesus." Now let's sing, "At The Cross At The Cross Where I First Found The Light, and the burden of my sins rolled away..."

****

But the real threat to Stand-Up Comedy itself comes from India: Laughter Yoga. You don't need to practice all these jokes, trying to get the timing right. All the endless rehearsal, the serious build-up that goes on and on, the perfectly timed punch line. No, all you need to do is just make these sounds while pretending to laugh!... ssiii... whh... sshhh... HAHAHA... HOHOHO... HRRIII! That's it! And people will laugh! You'll never have to get up there and suffer the terrible humiliation of bombing! Like I did for a year trying to tell *these jokes*!

****

When all else failed, I thought I could just talk in my perfect East Indian accent. Not even that worked, and it exposed my own racism. I had bombed already the first few jokes, so they must have thought, to top it all off, that I was just a racist pig. (Missionary's... not a little racist?) How could I tell them that I actually grew up speaking English like that as a child in Mumbai? My dad used to recite letters and essays he had received. Indian pastors would come over just to listen to him speak in forms of English that spanned the whole of India. I sat on my chair to the side and watched them laugh till they cried. One of his favorites was from an essay I had brought home from school in Mumbai. I think it was to be an example of how to write an essay. "The Horse:" (Accent Required... unless you're Indian.)

"The horse is a very noble quadruped, but when angry he will not do so. He is ridden on the spinal cord by the bridle. The driver simply divides his lower limbs across the saddle and drives his animal into the meadows. His head is attached to his body by a long protuberance called the neck. He has four legs; two are at the front side, and two follow immediately afterwards. These are the weapons by which he runs, and also extends his rear legs in a parallel direction toward his foe. He has the power to run as fast as he could. There are also horses of short sizes. They do the same as the others are generally doing."

But there was no laughing at the comedy clubs I went to. For some reason this stuff was not funny. So I quit. If I can't get people to laugh with my Horse story, forget it. I'll stick to poetry, for now. God will have to find a new way to teach me how to perform StandUp Comedy. I can wait and see.

About Atmosphere Press

Founded in 2015, Atmosphere Press was built on the principles of Honesty, Transparency, Professionalism, Kindness, and Making Your Book Awesome. As an ethical and author-friendly hybrid press, we stay true to that founding mission today.

If you're a reader, enter our giveaway for a free book here:

SCAN TO ENTER
BOOK GIVEAWAY

If you're a writer, submit your manuscript for consideration here:

SCAN TO SUBMIT
MANUSCRIPT

And always feel free to visit Atmosphere Press and our authors online at atmospherepress.com. See you there soon!

Milton Keynes UK
Ingram Content Group UK Ltd.
UKHW020036090524
442424UK00004B/266